the SHANTUNG
REVIVAL

1933

An Unedited Republication of the

Greatest Revival in Baptist Church History

D1059845

GLOBAL AWAKENING

THE SHANTUNG REVIVAL
Mary Crawford

Originally Published by
China Baptist Publication Society
Shanghai, China, 1933

Current Publication by
Global Awakening
Copyright 2005

Cover design by Chuck Schmidt
Printed in the United States of America

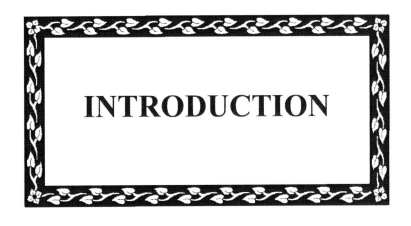

INTRODUCTION

I was called into the ministry at 18 in the midst of the Jesus Movement. My life and ministry are evidence of the lasting impact of that revival which swept across North America. My first encounter with revival was at our Baptist church where the average attendance was 125 people. Revival sparked first among the youth. I was the second of 11 young men to enter the ministry within a few months of the onset of that revival. 250 conversions were recorded during those six weeks when heaven visited earth in our small community. Those of us who are born into the kingdom of God, or called into the ministry, during a revival are forever ruined for anything less. Thirty-five years later my heart still cries for the manifest presence of God that is such an integral part of a revival atmosphere. More Lord! More Lord! More Lord.

I had the privilege of studying under Dr. Lewis Drummond at The Southern Baptist Theological Seminary in Louisville, Kentucky. It was through Dr. Drummond that I first heard of revival beyond my experience in 1970 when God powerfully moved in my small Baptist church. Through Dr. Drummond's class I learned how controversial, especially among the church, revival can be. I also discovered that revivals historically come at the church's low point when things look absolutely hopeless. It was amazing to hear how God would pierce through the darkness and accomplish more in one year than mans efforts had in the 25-50 years previous to a revival.

One of the most interesting revivals talked about by Dr. Drummond was The Shantung Revival, which took place in northern China in the early 1930's. Dr. Drummond believed The Shantung Revival to be, "the greatest revival in Baptist History". Dr. Drummond's teaching and passion for The Shantung Revival burned inside of me nearly twenty years before I pursued knowing more. The intrigue to further research this revival began in 1996 when I was given a book from someone who personally witnessed the revival. I became curious to know whether or not other Southern Baptist professors of evangelism would concur with Drummond's enthusiasm for the Shantung Revival. I was able to make connections with two professors of evangelism from the Southern Baptist Convention, both of whom agreed; The Shantung Revival had been the greatest in Baptist history.

I believe that we are living in a time prior to the greatest revival ever in Christian history. God is already bringing in a great harvest throughout the entire world. In many countries the church, the bride of Christ, is already experiencing revival. I have been privileged to be a part of revivals first hand, even across cultures. I have been honored to meet with revivalists, watch them minister, and minister with them. Men like Carlos Annacondia, Omar Cabrera, Claudio Freidzon, and Drs. Pablo Deiros and Carlos Mrarida of Argentina; Caesar Castianno of Columbia; Pastors

Paulo Garcia, Rene Terre-Nova, Jorge Markus of Uruguay; Pavel and Marina from Russia: etc. Despite all the revival atmospheres around the world that I've been chosen to work in, revival is not an easy thing to describe. James Burns' work <u>Revivals, Their Laws and Leaders</u>, is a classic on revival written in 1909 in England. Burns states,

> "No one can study, even superficially, the phenomena of revivals without being struck by the similarity of the effects produced upon those who come under their sway. Two of these stand out with startling vividness, and are common to all. (a) Every revival movement sees an awakening in the individual and in the Church of a deep sense of sin.... (b) The second characteristic effect produced by a revival movement is its wonderful outburst of joy....Whether the new-born gladness of heart finds its outlet in song or note, however, the gladness itself is never absent. In many it becomes so extreme that where the mind is ill-balanced it leads to dangerous excesses. Almost every revival is accompanied by outbursts of excitement, and by startling physical phenomena. Outbursts of physical anguish are followed by outbursts of uncontrollable joy, and the effect of these extreme emotions on ill-balanced natures is often disastrous. The spiritual value of a revival, however, is not to be negative because of the disastrous effect produced upon a certain number of excitable natures. Many who are on the outlook to cast opprobrium on all such movements select these excesses to prove the justice of their condemnations. They only prove the narrowness of their judgments, and show how,

by prejudice, movements which carry with them untold blessings to the race may be belittled by minds that fix upon the trivial, and by hearts that are bankrupt of lofty, spiritual emotions" (Burns, pp.23-25 1909 edition).

Burns also makes the following statement regarding the nature of revival,

"No less striking in their similitude are the phenomena which appear when the revival movement is set in motion. Immediately the voice of the leader is heard, vast forces, which seem hitherto to have been lying dormant, are awakened; the revival spreads with wings of fire, and huge numbers of men, women, and children are affected by it. Wherever it moves, and into whatever heart it enters, it creates an overwhelming sense of sin, and with sin's forgiveness an intense joy, a joy which expresses itself in jubilant song, and often in strange outbursts of feeling" (p.32 1909 edition)

Arthur Wallis, in his classic on revival, In the Day Of Thy Power, wrote,

"...revival is the divine intervention in the normal course of spiritual things. It is God revealing Himself to man in awful holiness and irresistible power. It is such a manifest working of God that human personalities are overshadowed and human programs abandoned" (p.20 1990 edition).

Could it be that our very programs have become idols to us, more important to us than the visitation of God? Perhaps the pastor of the largest Baptist Church in South Africa was correct when I heard him say during our visit to his church, "We cry for the Holy Spirit to come, we cry for revival, but when He does come we are quick to say, 'Now sit down on the back row and behave yourself'" (Quigney Baptist in East London). Allow me to paraphrase the pastor, "Our prayers are like saying, 'Here kitty, kitty, kitty.' And, the mighty lion of Judah appears and roars, causing great terror in us by his awesome power." It is this awesomeness of God, this very characteristic of God that insists He be the Lord and us His humble servants, that so scares pastors and people who like being in control. In times or revival God takes over His Church. But, not all are willing to yield His control,

> "The mighty operation of the Spirit will always uncover and draw forth into the open the antagonism of the natural or carnal mind which is 'enmity against God'. He whom God chooses to be an instrument in revival may expect to be a continual target for the malice of Satan, who never seem to lack willing hands or lips to do his work, in the church as well as out of it. Many know of the contribution of Jonathan Edwards to the New England revival of the seventeen hundreds; few know that he was ultimately compelled to resign from the church so signally blessed through his labors. ...So it was with Finney and many others. If we find a revival that is not spoken against, we

had better look again to ensure that it is revival"
(Wallis, pp.25-26).

It is good for North Americans to gain more
understanding of past and present revivals. When we
revisit the accounts of past revivals it makes us more open
to phenomena that isn't normally a part of life in the church,
yet we discover the same phenomena are in fact normal when
the church is in revival.

I want to have eyes to see and ears to hear what the
Spirit is saying to the churches. This book is a collection of
letters written by Southern Baptist missionaries to each other.
I hope this will cause you, and myself, to be more open to
the workings or the Holy Spirit. May we not find our voice
crying out against a move of God.

PREFACE

The compiler of this collection of testimonies does not in the least want to be considered as an "author," for there is almost no original composition in it. On the contrary it is composed of letters and testimonies written informally as friend to friend. These were written that Jesus Christ might be glorified. We ask your patience in reading not in a critical, but in a prayerful spirit. Not all the testimonies could be given, so selection had to be made of those which were representative. In the case of the healing of the eighteen year paralytic, and the case of little Samuel the facts were attested by missionaries; in the other cases the local Chinese Christians gave the evidence to the supervising missionary who saw the persons who had been healed. Should the question of healing in answer to prayer trouble you, we suggest a reading of A. J. Gordon's Ministry of Healing, a book which fell into the writer's hands after this book had been compiled; also an unprejudiced study of this subject from the Word of God. In fact had not this revival had the witness of the Spirit that it was in harmony with the Word of God, the leaders concerned would never have entered into it. Eph. 5:18.

Mary Crawford

Tsinan, China,
August, 1933.

"Not by might, nor by power,

but by my spirit, saith the Lord of hosts."

TABLE OF CONTENTS

CHAPTER	PAGE

CHAPTER ONE

A BORN AGAIN FOUNDATION

Jesus answered and said unto him, Verily, verily, I say unto thee, Except a man be born again he cannot see the kingdom of God. John 3:3.

The last days of April, 1929, all Shantung, and especially Southern Baptist circles, were shocked to hear that a missionary had been captured by pirates. Numbers of missionaries had been in the hands of bandits before, but this missionary was on her way from Tientsin to Hwanghsien to hold special meetings in our Mission there; several of us had traveled on the very boat that the pirates had taken. The horror seemed to reach out and touch us. Our prayers joined the prayer of other Christian circles that reached all the way to Norway, where cable had wired the news to the native country of the captured missionary. Afterwards Miss L. sent out circular reprints of Miss M's own letter telling of those twenty-three days in the hands of the pirates. Instead of days of misery, days of triumph and rejoicing were recorded. In her own words: "Just before daylight, I heard pistol shots all over the ship, and I knew immediately what we were in for. The words came to me: 'This is a trial of your faith.'" I remember the thrill of joy that went through me at the thought of it. I was immediately reminded of the word that I had been using much in years gone by, in Isaiah 41:10, and I will read it to you as I had been reading it down on the Honan plains, 'Fear not, Marie, for I am with thee; be not dismayed, Marie, for I am thy God; I will strengthen then thee, Marie, yea I will uphold thee, Marie, with the right hand of my righteousness.'"

Standing on the promises as given in the Book of Promises she went through the test of having a pistol pointed at her, plans to take her away with them, the intrusion of a vile bandit into her cabin, without a hair of her head being touched. Standing on the promises of the King of Kings she refused to obey the pirates orders, refused to eat the stolen food brought to her, refused to be frightened, and with perfect peace in her heart was not only kept in a miraculous way but witnessed to the two hundred passengers and fifty robbers, including hours of personal conversation on Salvation to the chief of the pirates himself.

But this missionary had another reputation, that of going about and asking people if they were born again. It was even reported that she asked missionaries themselves, "Have you been born again?" Some months after the pirate episode she held meetings at Hwanghsien, and imagine our surprise, and in spite of joy, shock, to hear that one of our own missionaries had been "born again." Later we shall hear her experience in her own words, but this was not the beginning of our spiritual hunger.

For several years there had been an increasing

hunger in the hearts of most of us to see more of the Power of the Holy Spirit in our work. We had been taught in our seminaries that if we ever got any souls saved it would be through the work of the Holy Spirit. We knew the doctrine of the Acts of the Apostles, but we were not experiencing it as we knew we should. After the Chinese Southern Army came in during the year 1928, \and so much of our work showed up as "hay and stubble" most of us were willing to "humble ourselves under the mighty hand of God that He might exalt us in due season." Miss L. and other missionaries who had heard Miss M's testimonies during the time of refugeeing in Chefoo, were glad and willing to have her come into their Missions with the pointed question of, "Have you been born again?"

But let us hear from one who truly faced the question during the Hwanghsien meetings. As far as "natural sweetness which may exist quite apart from grace," the writer has never met a more unselfish character. During the year together at Language School Miss——— was very popular because of her sterling character and devoted service to others. She had had a real call to service in China; she had been inspired time and again by Christ's teachings. But let us hear her own words:

"I've tried to figure it all out why I missed the way of salvation. I know I was reared with strictness as to religious duties, but if I was depending on 'works,' as one friend told me it appeared to her, it was without any conscious idea of it.

I really enjoyed church going, memorizing Bible verses, and had answers to prayer. It was not, as I once thought, because I did not hear the Gospel, for I did hear it, and I knew I had sins, a rather deep sense of it beginning early. I feel that when times of conviction came that sin (of stealing 25 cents from our next door neighbor and covering it with a lie when my mother questioned me) was the one that God wanted me to confess, and just tell my mother that I had lied to her, but I refused to listen to Him. I just begged Him to forgive me and make me forget that sin. In giving this testimony I do not mean to intimate that any one was to blame for my failure to be saved earlier. My home training was careful and I was taught much about God and about the sinfulness of sin. Many verses of scripture were memorized for which I have been profoundly grateful to my Mother and Sunday School teachers. There was one time at our church when the Cross of Christ was so lifted up I felt that I must talk to that minister about my soul's condition. At that time I satisfied myself with the assurance that I was a church member and therefore saved. At the timed I joined the church I was thirteen. I attended revival meetings at another B. church in our city; the invitation for sinners to hold up their hands annoyed me, and I asked a girl by me, "Who are sinners?" she replied, "Those not in the church." With this I held up my hand but had no idea of confessing the sin that was in my heart. Many a time I had heard God's voice telling me to confess my sin but the fear of punishment and later, fear of being known as a thief held me back. I joined the church and was baptized but the sin remained. In the baptismal pool I silently cried to God, "Let this water wash that sin away." It had become a bother to me and I do praise the Lord He kept on reminding me of it till I yielded to His leading in confessing and making restitution. There were many other sins, but stealing from a neighbor twenty-five cents with which I bought candy and covering over the whole with a lie, which my Mother believed, was the sin that kept me so many years from getting right with God. When Miss P. was here she asked if we had real communion with the Lord, and urged us to get alone with the Lord till we felt His presence. I did this and felt it, but beginning to be afraid, jumped up and ran away, for I could not bear that Presence. I knew then that it meant returning that money to the woman. I told Him that I would confess to my Mother when I went on furlough. Some peace came then. But when I went on furlough I could not summon up the necessary courage. All this time I had not doubted my salvation, or I hardly believe that I would have come back to China. I had been back just a year when miss M. came. Something in me did not want her to come. But one day a fellow missionary gave me the thought that the thing to do was to pray, "Lord, send a revival, and begin in me."

When the meeting began I hoped the speaker would not ask me the question, "Are you born-again?" I sat near the front in the foreign meetings to be sure she would not detect any lack in me. O, my deceitful heart, when I should have been eager for the light which I did not have! She asked us missionaries to help her in personal work by asking the Chinese if they were 'born-again'. This I did one morning after Chinese service, and the question choked me, and my heart bore witness, 'You're not born-again yourself, how can you ask that question?' This was early in the meetings; by Wednesday I was very miserable, but tried to keep happy and singing, consoling myself that if I could sing I knew I was saved. Wednesday p.m., I went through a period of questioning. M. was at home and I talked to her, whether she answered or not I do not know, but she did not give me any comfort, for which I praise the Lord. It was a series such as this: 'I think I'm saved.', 'How could I be here if I were not saved.', 'I hope I am saved,' 'Well, I guess I am saved,' 'Well, I ought to be,' and so on. Then I went to work and to the afternoon meeting. I had planned to ask Miss M. to walk with me and put the facts of my case before her so as to make her think I was talking about someone else. When I asked her she indifferently replied, 'No, I am going with someone else.' I went home and felt that there was no help, ate a little supper and to the hospital for prayers with the nurses. One of the nurses asked me what was the difference between 'believe and be saved' and be 'born-again.' (Believe can be used in a sense such as to believe the fact of Christ's advent and teachings without the work of grace in a heart changed by Him.) I answered, "'You will find out later.' I went home, M. was out; I was in the big house alone. I knelt by the bed and prayed, 'Lord, I don't know whether I'm saved or not but you know; I want to be right with you and with man, please show me what is wrong.' My sins came before me like darkness, and I cried, 'What can I do?' Just then the burden rolled away and the Light of Salvation shone in my soul. I saw my sins and I saw the Cross. Such joy flooded my being but it was only a moment before the temptation, 'It cannot last, such joy as this,' but then came the blessed assurance in Rom. 8 that 'neither death nor life, nor angels nor principalities nor—height nor depth nor any other creature should be able to *separate me* from the Love of God which is in Christ Jesus, our Lord." Quickly I jumped up to run down stairs to hunt a sheet of precious promises printed in Chinese. I looked up the promises in English and wrote them in the back of my Bible. They were the most precious words I had ever know? Then I took paper and pencil and began writing a letter home confessing how far short I had fallen of all they had believed me to be and sending back a dollar to pay for the twenty-five cents that I had stolen when a child. Then and there the Bible became a new book to me; I was a new creation in Christ Jesus. I knew that as God revealed my sins to me I would do what He suggested about restitution. I was full of joy and peace about my salvation, but after meeting with God I wanted every pretence and wrong dealing with man made straight. Some things were hard, but He made it harder not to do this. he showed me many things and it has brought me joy as one thing after another has been made right with man."

This worker went on in joy and witnessing, became very earnest in soul winning, had no other desire but to see souls saved, and has since received the fullness of the Holy Spirit.

It seems needless to say that the Revival was born out of prayer groups who were asking definitely for revival. Several stations had prayer bands, but we have space to mention only the one with which we were closely connected.

For years there had been a prayer group of women in Tsinan. As far back as 1925 there was one home where choice friends were invited to dinner, the place cards were prayer pledges, reading, "O Lord revive thy church, beginning in me." In the summer of 1930 a group of five hungry missionaries went to Summer Conference hunting a new experience in the Lord. Miss L. never stopped stressing in prayer and laying upon the hearts of the others the fact that there were seventy off "dead churches" in the North China Association. During the summer a definite prayer list was made on which it was agreed to pray for revival in Tsinan, Tsining and Hwanghsien. In the fall of 1930 Miss M. came for meetings in Tsinan. The leaders were ready and willing to have the church exposed to the question, "Have you been born again?"

Right here I want to say that none of these "Born

Again" revivals had the least taint of sensationalism about them. The singing was the usual mediocre singing of the congregation, there was no advertising other than announcements. Miss M. herself is one of the quietest speakers I ever heard, but any one with any discernment at all could see and feel that she was depending upon the promises of God in a remarkable way, and most especially upon the promise given in the Gospel of John 16:8, "And when He (the Holy Spirit) is come, He will reprove the world of sin, and of righteousness, and of judgment." He, Himself, the Holy Spirit, will convict of sin. The Word of God concerning sin was given in a quiet, unassuming manner, and it became "quick and powerful, and sharper than any two-edged sword, piercing even to the dividing asunder of soul and spirit, and of the joints and marrow, and is a discerner of the thoughts and intent of the heart."

"But was not Grace and the Cross preached?" you ask. Yes, God's grace had been preached for years, but so many had accepted God's grace as an outside coat of whitewash, and had covered their sins in their naturally prepared hearts.

To continue the account of the Tsinan Revival which we had the privilege of attending, the members of the congregation were exposed to what the Bible says concerning definite sins, one sin discussed at each session—not the fact that we are all sinners jumbled into one sermon. For example: After the foundation fact "Ye must be born again"

had been well-rubbed in; one day the sin of Hate, and what
the Bible says about Hate, what Hate does to men's hearts,
and the freedom that comes when Christ changes the heart
and hate is forgiven; then the next session the sin of Lies,
then the sin of Stealing, Covetousness, the whole decalogue,
yes, even Adultery. With the boldness and power which
only comes from a heart continually cleansed by the Blood
of Jesus, what the Bible teaches about each sin was given,
in a vivid, forceful manner. At the close of each session
the speaker took her stand at the door and put the question
"Have you been born again?" to individuals as they met
her. The evasion, the doubt, the conviction was terrible.
In some places, if there was a back door, the victims under
conviction would escape through it. With all the preaching
of what the Bible says about Sin, there came the most terrible
conviction of the Righteousness and Holiness of God, with
the surety of judgment. All the time there was definite prayer,
especially for the "key person" in the church, who happened
to be the young pastor's wife. She was a young woman of
vivid personality, graduate of our Mission High School,
several years of hospital training, and also several years in
the Seminary. She knew her Bible, but it come to light that
she was on the prayer lists of several groups of missionaries
who felt that she had not been saved. But let us hear her
experience as given by herself:

"When Miss M. asked me, 'Have you been born
again?', I tried to assure her and myself that an experience of

faith in prayer for my husband's sickness about two week's before was a born again experience, but before the week was over I knew better. Day after day as the messages were given as to how God regards hate, lying, stealing, in fact all the sins covered by the ten commandments, I knew myself to be undone before God. My sins were spread out before me and I knew I must go to the Cross for confession and forgiveness. I knew my Bible well, and could handle it in a mechanical way, but that could not wipe away the sin of hating my first baby because I wanted a diploma more than a baby. In knowing my sins of hate and discord, the truth of I Jno. 3:15 cut like a "two edged sword." But I could not surrender my pride and stubbornness till the last day of the meeting, and Oh! the floods of joy and peace as assurance of the forgiveness of sins came. I gave my testimony and confessed my sins before the whole church because I felt that as a pastor's wife I had caused them all to stumble. O, friends, is it possible that education and Seminary training have taken the place of a real work of grace in your heart? Are you a new creation in Christ Jesus?"

The True Light School had two attractive young women teachers, and we all had thought that they were converted. To an American, Miss L. especially was very attractive. She has good clear-cut features, wavy hair, a generous mouth, and eyes that speak for energy and sincerity. Her personality is as glowing and promising as the first rays of the morning sun. But when the convicting power of God's Word spoke to her, she saw herself a lost sinner. Impulsive and open-hearted, she was the first to go under deep conviction; the first to have a clear-cut, "born again" experience. But let us hear her own experience:

"At first the meetings made no impression on me, and I thought that Miss M. had no right to ask me, "Have you been born again?" Then I came under deep conviction and saw myself unclean before the Living God. My pride, deceit, worldliness, and hate weighed as a burden in my heart. God's Word in Rom. 1:28-32 and II Tim. 3:2-4 became a living picture to my heart. My own righteousness became as "filthy rags" before a Holy God. Although I had been a nominal Christian from childhood, and had always been in Mission Schools, my heart had experienced no change. Several times I had been inspired by good preaching, and had determined not to sin, determined to be good, but I kept on sinning. although we had Bible lessons in school, we only read the Bible because we had to. Then in the last years of High School anti-foreign propaganda reached us, and I came to believe that the Church was an "Imperial Machine," that prayer was empty, the Bible written by men only, not the least understanding of the second birth. I was not the least afraid of God. Then suddenly I went under deep conviction and saw myself a lost sinner. I was physically limp, had no hope; knew that the "wages of sin is death." When I had no hope, the word of the Lord in John 3:36 came to me. I wanted the life that Jesus gives, and knelt before the Lord and gave my sins to Him one by one. Then I took the promise of I John 1:9 and let the Holy Spirit do His work in my heart, received the new life that Jesus gives. October 11, 1930 I was "born again." Oh, what joy.' In all my twenty-three years I had never been so happy. My feet could not stay on the ground, my heart was so light. Then I knew that Jesus was a Living Lord, a Lord who frees sinners. Within a month I heard the voice of the Lord saying, "Follow Me." And so I have, going to the lost around me with the message of John 4:14. I believe that the New Birth is a necessity. The Life that Jesus only can give is a living, vital, glorious fact."

Miss L. has since gone through the test of opposition from her family. Her father being dead, her brother has control and he was determined she should not do anything so foolish as follow a life of faith, but tried to make her compromise with a good position in "Social Gospel" work. But nothing other than vital work in the "born again" revival satisfied her. Then her brother tried making a worldly marriage for her, but prayer prevailed, and she has lived to see her brother change his attitude, and himself experience the New Birth. She is now in a Seminary for Bible study and looks forward to pioneer work when she graduates.

The other teacher, Miss Li, was more reserved, old-fashioned and of the official class. The first meetings could not break down her reserve, but a second week on what the Bible teaches about sin, broke her down completely. In her own words, "Conviction settled down on my heart as a cloud that could not be borne. I almost had to run to a Christian worker and ask her to help me pray." The New Birth freed her from her sins, and she has since been an open-hearted radiant soul-winner in the school.

But these are only a few outstanding examples of the first fruits of the revival. As one missionary wrote: "We have suddenly been brought to our senses as a result of Miss M.'s messages on sin. Our best (?) church members have been brought under deep conviction of sin. They have come weeping and confessing sins, which they have kept hidden all these years. So we have been having an in-gathering of 'Born again' ones from among the church members as well as the outsiders." She also adds that not one of the deacons of the church was clear on the New Birth. After the first meeting they and the teachers began to try to teach and preach the New Birth, but soon showed that they did not know what they were talking about. Some said that one could not know till death, but the bright, happy faces of those who had been freed convicted him. There began a searching of the Scriptures and a confession of sins that brought assurance. One deacon was so anxious about his condition that he said that it made no difference whether he had his supper or not—he wanted to bring his Bible and get straight. When asked if he believed all the Bible he had no difficulty there, but when asked if his name was written in the Book of Life, he just said, "No, I am not sure, but because I don't think my sins are open and confessed."

Now I will quote in full from a letter as to how the first messages on sin struck two churches.

"MY DEAR PRAYER-HELPERS:

Thank God in answer to prayer we have had eight wonderful days here. It truly has been a time of reaping with joy. I found many hungry prepared hearts here. It was easy work preaching to them.

K. is only half an hour away from K. . . . . . .by railroad. Some of the workers here went to the meetings there, the leading evangelist among them. He had for some time been on the point of despair on account of the hopelessness of the work. He himself is a fine man, reborn. He seemed to realize that most of the church members, more than a thousand, had only been converted to Christianity and not to Christ. At the first meeting at————he seemed to get the help he needed both for himself and for his work. Tears of joy were streaming down his face when he discovered he had a part in helping two evangelists into the kingdom. One evangelist and a teacher came back from K. saved. They were on fire, and the Lord has greatly used them in meetings here. They have been doing personal work all the time.

During the two weeks between the meetings at K. and here, a prayer meeting was held three times a day for all the worker in the district, and the Lord did indeed prepare their hearts for the meetings during the days of prayer.

Besides the church members about fifty workers have attended the meetings, and with the leading evangelist on the right side there was no opposition. He who has come into the world to convict of sin, was in our midst from the very beginning. Convicted, burdened sinners were privately and quietly helped through, by those who were already saved.

One young man tried to deceive himself and others; he insisted he was saved. He was a worker. But He could not deceive the Holy Spirit. One night the healthy young man was struck down in the court yard. He had to be carried in, stiff and blue and cold. Friends burdened for his soul were kneeling at his side crying for mercy. The missionary called into his ears, "Confess your sins quickly"! And as soon as he could open his mouth he just poured out his black sins, and stood on his feet again, a forgiven sinner. Praise the dear Lord, the Saviour of all sinners!

Several others have had God's hand on them in the same way. One old, hardened sinner, also a worker, and a much prayed for man, one evening could not possibly keep his seat. In spite of himself he had to get up, he had to go to the front, and he just had to pour out a life of black sins before them all. No public confessions had been made before. He just confessed,—he had to—but seemed hard and cold and untouched through it all, and the atmosphere of the place seemed suddenly changed, the church seemed filled with evil spirits. But the next day he was a broken man, tears streaming down his face. He seemed to be set free, but he has many things to put right.

Everything otherwise has been so quiet. But for a wonderful spirit of prayer and an occasional testimony now and again, no one dropping in would think we were in the midst of a revival. The sweet, "Abba, Father" that has seemed to come from the depth of the hearts of many, has shown one how lovely it has been to "come home." It sounds like the Lord of the harvest is calling out laborers for His own work. Whenever it comes out in prayer, I feel like we are on Holy Ground. Some of these friends have asked for a an interview today. Oh! for more men and women with a Divine call upon them for the work. May God forgive us for all the men-called workers in China.

"Almost all of our workers are saved now," said one of the missionaries this morning. I could only answer, "Don't be too sure of them. By their fruits shall they be known. But I do realize that a real work of the Holy Spirit has been done in the hearts of many of them. They have been helping each other through. It was almost comical to hear one of the evangelists tell how the goat boy had helped him. And a very clever teacher went and woke up a colporter, who can hardly read to come help him.

Glory to God and to our Lord Jesus Christ and to the Holy Spirit, for all the wonders He allowed us to see.

And thanks to all you dear friends, who so faithfully stand by in prayer. God bless you all richly."

"Yours in the ministry of reconciliation,"

Another worker writes:

"We had been praying for three years that this special worker should come to Pingtu. God truly sent her to us, and the revival for which we have been praying, has begun. A large audience of pastors, evangelists, workers, Christians and students filled the large church. As the teaching on sin from the Bible was given, the Holy Spirit carried the message to every heart. A holy quietness filled the church so that all could hear every word.

Testimonies from saved ones in recent meetings at other places helped much. A well-educated educator, graduate from an American college, gave a good testimony. He said he had been a "nao tzu" (brain) Christian for ten years, then he was saved in the meetings in T . . . . An evangelist from L. and also a cook, gave their testimonies.

I wish I could yell you in detail, of all that were saved during the meetings, but space forbids, so I only tell a few of the outstanding ones.

We felt that Mr. H. was saved and were so happy that he had come and was sitting near the front, listening so well. When the speaker asked him face to face if he were saved he said, "Yes." She remarked to us that he had a "dead man's eyes." As he listened, and the Holy Spirit worked, he began to doubt his salvation; did not feel that his evidence was sufficient. He felt that he must know. He said he was anxious, and asked a friend to pray earnestly for him. This friend prayed and he prayed and struggled. Finally he said, "Lord I will do anything you tell me to do, if I can only get peace." The Holy Spirit brought all his sins before him and he confessed them to the Lord, but God told him to confess them in the presence of his friend. Satan said, "There is no need to lose face by confessing all." He replied that face was not to be compared with eternal life. Peace and joy came, and a new light shown from his eyes.

. . . . Right here, in parentheses, let us follow up this completely changed man. Two years have passed since this letter I am quoting was written. This Mr. H. was a doctor and was leading a comfortable life in his home town. He so felt the passion for souls that he turned his medicine shop over to a clerk, and for two years now has given his time to country evangelistic work with the local missionary. Week in and week out, in uncomfortable quarters in the country places he is giving his life and energy to leading revival meetings. He and the missionary have seen as many as one hundred a week saved. He went into this work not expecting and not caring for a salary, but the revival has so worked in other places that a Christian doctor who works in an R.R. hospital is now paying this man's salary. He, Mr. H . . . has since been filled with the Spirit and is used in a great way . . . .

Going back to the letter we were quoting:

"Another interesting case is that of an old classics teacher in the Girls' School. He had already joined the church as a nominal Christian. He is the old-style scholar, has studied both Chinese and Western history quite extensively. He had also read his Bible through and was interested in the truth therein. When Miss M. started her meetings he felt that she must have some hypnotic power and that the personal workers were aiding her by asking people if they were saved. The third day he decided that she knew psychology. The fifth day he felt he must know whether there is a God or not, and whether he was a sinner or not. He thought he had no sins. At two o'clock that night he had to get up and pray. As he prayed his sins came before him. He got a piece of paper and wrote them down, then he doubted, thinking that this was his own thinking and that the Holy Spirit had nothing to do with it. He wanted to be sure, so he prayed something like this: "God, if you are God, and if Miss M. is not doing her work in her own strength, and if the blood that Jesus shed on the Cross can wash away my sins, and if these sins brought before me are the conviction of the Holy Spirit, then I'll confess all and ask you to give me peace; then I'll know you are God." Peace came, and with it assurance that God is the true, living God. At the next service he led in prayer.

. . . . . Again, we just must follow up the old man in the two years of revival, for a year late he found that God not only forgives sin but has the power to save from sinning, for he gave up his beloved tobacco because it hurt his Christian testimony. Now he teaches during the week and goes out after sinners on Sunday afternoon. We saw him sitting in the nightly Bible study group just radiant, and chuckling with joy as his position in the resurrected Lord is being revealed to him by Bible study. He was leading the group to pray for fifty souls to give the Lord for a Christmas present. Such a different prayer from the first midnight one! . . . . .

"One of the younger teachers in the Boys School was under such deep conviction that he thought the earth would swallow him up. Praying friends helped him to find peace at the foot of the Cross. Those who had such clear-cut experiences were used to help their friends almost immediately.

The leading woman teacher was gloriously saved; in her testimony she said, "I know the gate to heaven is narrow; I know there is a definite time when the blood is applied." She was used in bringing the other women teachers into a clear, "born-again" experience.

My heart ached as I saw one of the oldest Bible women confessing her sins to God. It was hard; but I thank God she is a new creature in Christ Jesus now. She had to send some conscience money back where she had worked.

The revival is going on still, and we feel that this is only the beginning. Souls are being saved daily."

Another letter, written in 1931:

DEAR FRIENDS:

You who have been praying for the meetings in Laiyang will be happy to know that the Holy Spirit worked in convicting and saving power.

. . . .As soon as Mr. Li reached Laichow and found some of his friends rejoicing in the new birth, a sword was thrust into his own heart. He knew their liberty and joy was something which he had never experienced, and with a burdened heart he wept and prayed a good portion of the night, and returned with us to Laiyang the next day, a miserable man indeed. The first service increased his misery but the Holy Spirit completed the work which He had begun and on the evening of the second day, after having honestly laid his sins before the Lord, he was released.

The cook of one of the missionaries was gloriously saved during the Laichow meetings. He went to Laiyang to cook for our party, arriving just before the first service there was closed. He formerly lived in Laiyang and was a faithful member of the church and well known by the congregation. When he led the closing prayer all knew from the prayer that he was marvelously changed. One man with a hungry heart followed him home and sat in the kitchen inquiring about the "new life" while the cook prepared dinner. After every service, six or eight men, evangelists among the number, gathered about him wanting to know how they, too, might receive such joy. One day in his prayer he said, "'Lord I thank you that now I am not I.' A truer statement was never made, for indeed he is a new creature in Christ Jesus. His seventeen-year-old brother came into the city to be with him, and was soon made miserable enough to confess his sins and receive saving faith.

"A number of men were ready to receive the truth, and after a few days of awakening, followed by condemnation, a number were born again. One evening during prayer service they could contain their misery no longer, and a number broke out into confession before God. One was saved that night, and others one by one came into the joy of forgiveness. Another evangelist, named Li, a big, fine-looking man, had a disturbed countenance after the first day, and showed that his burden of sin was growing heavier day by day; but next to the last day we went into the church and saw a new man. In his testimony he said that he had never before realized that he had any sin whatever. He was not afraid to meet God because he was unconscious of being unprepared. As he listened to the truth day by day he saw himself a hell-deserving sinner and was willing to come by the way of confession and self abasement . . . . .

Pray for Mr. C., the leading evangelist, who insisted that the would not be turned away from heaven, because he had preached more than twenty years."

Perhaps the reader is beginning to have some questions, such as, "Isn't all this confession Catholic?"

"Why all the stress on sin?" Then there are always some circles who dub any revival "Emotional," and continue in the same old ruts that are 'so safe and sane' and where nothing ever happens.

In answer to the first question we want to say that confession was not stressed and public confession was not allowed except in a few extreme cases already mentioned, or where confession concerned the public. But the speaker was resting on the promise in John 16:8. He, (the Holy Spirit) when He is come, will convict the world in respect of sin, and of righteousness and of judgment." A. V. Praying with a personal worker was encouraged because it frees. The writer knows because of personal experience. It is a living doctrine that works. It is as old as Job. In personal interviews only Bible verses were given that the convert might stand on God's word for assurance. After conviction and confession, the stress was upon the cleansing power of the shed blood of Jesus Christ. There was never a message given that did not also point the way to the Cross. The messages were mostly given in circles where God's grace had been preached for years.

As for the second question, "Why all the stress on sin?", if you had heard some of the sins confessed you would not have to ask. Perhaps the question will clear up in the next chapter. You would have been grieved to have heard the answers which the "best" church members gave to the question, "Have you been born again?" Some of the of characteristic answers were: "I've preached for years." "I've been baptized." "I have dreamed so and so." Or, "One cannot know till death."

As for the question "Emotional?" The only answer is, "No." From the letters you must already realize that it was a work of deep faith, relying upon the convicting power of the Holy Spirit. In the first revival meetings in Shantung, there was very poor singing, no altar calls, no chance given for public confession, but only the pressing home of the quiet question, "Have you been born again!"

CHAPTER TWO

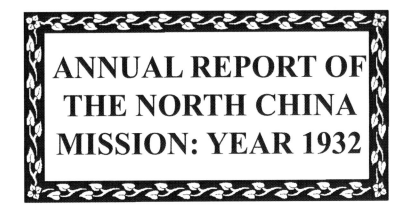

ANNUAL REPORT OF THE NORTH CHINA MISSION: YEAR 1932

"Behold, I will do a new thing; now it shall spring forth; shall ye not know it? I will even make a way in the wilderness, and rivers in the desert."

NEW THINGS IN N. CHINA BRIEFLY EXPRESSED:

HWANGHSIEN:

"In the revival here in Hwanghsien last spring the N. China Baptist Theological Seminary and Bible School; came in for a great blessing. Everyone of the faculty got a distinct blessing, and nearly everyone of them was filled with the Holy Spirit. It has made a new school."

Evangelistic Work: "It is a new day for us. Every month or so, all the churches and out-stations have had special revivals held by missionaries or special evangelists, and the results have been greater than many previous years put together.———One blessed result of the outpouring of the Spirit is that He sends people to ask the Way."

Warren Memorial Hospital: "The hospital was mightily blessed during the spring. Many of the personnel were saved and some filled with the fullness of the Spirit."

Tsingtao:

"During this week of prayer in the Tsingtao Church, daily testimony is being given by Mr. Chao Deh San, one of the brightest mission pupils our early schools ever knew, who has spent his life in Government service, building Rail and Motor Roads. In his sixtieth year, after forty years in the wilderness; he confessed and put away his sins, and is now visiting the cities where he worked and sinned, testifying to the saving power of Christ."

Tsinan:

"More people have been saved the past year than perhaps in any year in the history of the work here. The churches have never been on such a high plane spiritually as now. Practically all the preachers, teachers, Bible women and missionaries have had a blessed experience in the deeper things of the Holy Spirit, and have more real victory and power than they had ever known before."

Tsining:

"Our people have become of one heart and mind in the Lord Jesus, as never before.——We feel that the year has led us on to new spiritual heights."

HARBIN:

"A new church was organized, and this with fighting in hearing distance. This group also doubled the size of their gospel hall in spite of demoralized business conditions."

LAICHOW-LAIYANG:

"This has truly been one of our very best years spent in China.——It is absolutely beyond the power of human tongues to express the sheer joy and rapture of this new, marvelous, intimate fellowship into which we were brought with the glorified Redeemer Himself.——On that night there began the most wonderful revival ever witnessed in that little church."

CHEFOO:

"In place of having difficulty in finding teachers who would be willing to suffer the reproach of being superstitious and unpatriotic, we have had to refuse applicants sufficient to re-staff the schools."

PINGTU:

"God has been adding daily to His church. The

general estimate is that three thousand souls have been saved this year. There have been about nine hundred baptisms, with others waiting. "The Acts of the Holy Spirit "are being reacted in a remarkable way right here in our midst."

A PERSONAL MISSIONARY LETTER TELLING OF THE REVIVAL
IN THE NORTH CHINA MISSION.

I.

Chefoo, Shantung Province, China, July 4, 1932.

DEAR BROTHER PASTOR, BRETHREN AND SISTERS:

In our annual Missionary Conference here these last few days someone exclaimed: "Oh, that our Baptist people at home could hear and see what has come to our ears and eyes these past months!" "Yes," replied another, "how they would rejoice with us! And should the Holy Spirit bless them as He has many of us and our Chinese brethren and sisters, the debt on foreign missions would be wiped out in a short while!" That you may enter into this joy with us, pray for greater blessings upon us, and for a real revival in the churches of our Southern Baptist convention, the writer was asked to prepare one or more letters to be sent by individual missionaries to pastors and others at home.

It may not be generally known that perhaps the greatest revival in the history of Southern Baptists in North China is now being experienced in many Chinese churches of our North China Mission. This has come as a result of EARNEST PRAYER, FAITH IN GOD, BIBLE TEACHING, and MUCH PREACHING on sin and kindred subjects. Numbers of

Christians and churches are being revived; restitution of money is being made; tithes of the Lord held back are being brought forward; sins confessed to God and to those who have been wronged; sick are being healed; devils cast out; men and women, boys and girls are preaching with a power hitherto not known; hundreds are crying for mercy and are being saved. The devil is also at work, but there is great blessing and rejoicing in many places. Missionaries and Christians are marveling at the wonderful works of God.

During a quiet series of meetings held in Tsinan, the capital of Shantung, people were led to examine their hearts, for the searching, message of the leader was: "Are you saved; have you been born again?" This simple question, asked publicly and privately throughout North China and Manchuria, has put many to thinking. Church members apparently unsaved—and leaders among them—confessed their sins, and were marvelously saved. Then other meetings were held in Tsinan. Each time the people moved closer to the Lord. Joy following the forgiveness of sins, love for Christ and concern for the lost took possession of the saved, and has spread like fire there and elsewhere in that region.

There were wonderful results among the students of the Shantung Christian University. This fine institution adjoins the Baptist compound at Tsinan, a hundred being saved the past year. Many were led to the Lord by a professor, also blessed in these meetings. Missionaries, pastors and others, willing formerly to work only as average Christians, became dissatisfied, put themselves on the altar anew, were filled with the Spirit, and now see the Lord in a different way. They have a new joy in the Lord and a vigor in their work hitherto not known. The revival there, as at other places, began with the leaders. Some missionaries found that they were not without sins, and so did other leaders. These confessed their sins to God and to those whom they had offended, even though this often meant "loss of face" (embarrassment). The result is that many are being saved.

God's power came mostly during prayer services, while studying earnestly the Holy Spirit and His work by men and women who met separately in rooms of the Church. People were broken up and wept for their sins. There were then special manifestations of the Spirit's power and great rejoicing. Nothing like it has been seen in old Tsinan. A young man, for years only a nominal Christian, came forward confessing his sins and placed on the table ten dollars which he had wrongfully received. Others also brought money which did not belong to them, and a number brought funds which should have been given to the Lord. A wealthy man, who had been only an average Christian, has become a great leader, and so have others. These have now gone out in the city and country churches, some of which were almost dead, to conduct meetings. The churches are being revived and many saved. The big gospel tent, unused for two years for lack of funds and workers, is now being taken over the country by earnest Christians, these bearing the expense and doing the preaching. The Tsinan Church now pays all its pastor's salary, supports three theological students in the Seminary, and has made other advances in self-support.

Speaking of the revival in the country districts of the Tsinan field, one of the missionaries said: "Our country work has been revolutionized. Last year we decided to discontinue work at two places and go on to others because the people seemed hardened, but now it is different. The few old Christians there have been revived. They have power and are now doing the preaching themselves. It would all seem a dream did we not realize it is real. A man at another place thought himself saved, but then realized he was lost and prayed in great agony for forgiveness. His is now saved, and also his wife. They have revolutionized their village. Another layman who was saved recently has rented a place to be used as a preaching hall. Numerous Christians have confessed their sins and gotten right with God. Unsaved who scoffed at the gospel are now coming for salvation. What we call the 'Model Church,' recently built by the people themselves in one of the villages, a result of the revival, is the best building in the town, and is crowded. From fifty to sixty are awaiting baptism there."

Thus God's Spirit is doing wonderful things in the capital of Shantung and elsewhere in our Mission as a result of earnest prayer, preaching and teaching of His Work. Pray that the fire may continue to spread, and that God will likewise bless His people in the homeland.

ANOTHER LETTER FROM ONE OF YOUR MISSIONARIES

TELLING OF GOD'S REVIVING POWER IN CHINA.

II.

DEAR BROTHER PASTOR, BRETHREN AND SISTERS:

You will be interested to hear of the moving of God's Spirit in the Schools of the North China Mission as reported recently at our annual Mission Conference in Chefoo.

During a prayermeeting at one of the schools in Hwanghsien a boy, so convicted of sin that his body became rigid, fell against one of his teachers, crying aloud for mercy. He was told to pray to God, but begged that they carry him home, for he thought he would surely die. (Chinese all want to die at home.) He was terribly afraid, for the devil had led him into great sin. He was laid upon a bench and several of his friends—teachers and students—bowed close beside him, praying earnestly for him. Either the hand of the Lord, or the consciousness of sin, bore heavily upon him, for he felt that life was being crushed out of him. After a half hour of great agony, his body rigid, he cried aloud: "O, God, if you will not kill me, I will confess my sins!" And then for an hour he poured out his heart to God. He confessed the deepest and blackest sins, such as had never been heard in that school. He hated and wanted to take the life of a classmate who had kindly loaned him money simply because this friend was better off than he. His hatred of the rich had become so great that he wanted to destroy them and seize what they possessed, for he had become a real communist ("red") at heart. He asked student friends to forgive him because he had tried to convince them that there is no God. Among other terrible things, he confessed to God how he had sworn to kill every person in the world if there be a chance, and then that because the world is not right he determined to go to heaven and kill God himself! But God graciously forgave him and he, as did others, received peace and salvation. This school has never before had such spiritual blessing.

"In our school new hearts and new lives have been born in girls whose only heritage was depravity of generations of idolatrous ancestry. We rejoice that many have been led of the Spirit into a deeper experience and walk in Christ Jesus." So goes the report of the Girls' Boarding School at Tsinan, in another part of this Province of thirty-five million souls, the vast majority of whom are yet unsaved. This report, read at our annual Mission Conference in Chefoo, continues: "During the year the girls themselves organized an evangelistic band and on Sunday afternoons have gone out preaching in the nearby villages. This spring, after the hot weather began, a group walked five miles and came home with their faces beaming because they had experienced the joy of witnessing for their Saviour. The read was dusty and the day uncomfortably hot, but this little group of school girls sang praises to their God as they walked, and spent their rest time by the roadside praying for the souls of those to whom they were taking the gospel. When they returned at twilight with shining eyes, and voices still joyous with praise, the report continues, we found that during the whole long hot afternoon the girls had not bothered about the comfort of a single drink of water, but exclaimed: 'It was the best trip we ever took!" Faculty and students have made great progress in spiritual growth in this school. The principal rejoices that the chief aim and ideal of the students is the spiritual uplift of the students and the salvation of their people.

A revival in the church at Tsining resulted in a new era in the Boys' and Girls' Schools there. Due to reduction of funds from America the Middle School departments had to be closed and these pupils sent to the Presbyterian Schools, but the enrollment increased nevertheless. "The tone of the schools is so fine as a result of the revival that our hearts overflow with rejoicing to God for rich blessings from Him this year, for never was the spiritual atmosphere of the schools so high. Many have received great spiritual blessing, and, on going home, were looking forward to a summer of witnessing to parents, relatives and friends." These are extracts from the Girls' School and Woman's Training School at Laichowfu.

The Boys' Middle School at Pingtu rejoices that all graduates this year are Christians, one an earnest preacher and others outstanding disciples. There was a serious cut in funds and other difficulties, but again, we are reminded, the greatest feature of the work was the spiritual revival this year, a blessing to students and teachers. A number took part in the students' Sunday preaching on the streets and in outlying districts. Another report says: "God's boundless grace poured out upon us in increasing fullness this year, the best and richest in the long history of our institution."

And now read these lines from the Effie Sears Memorial School for Girls, located at Pingtu, where the revival began: "No longer a school, but a POWER-HOUSE, preparing bands of soul-winners, no longer 'hireling teachers,' but men and women watching prayerfully the spiritual growth of each student; no longer simply a mission school, but 'everything for God's glory! Praise His holy name, for He is head of this school!" This note rings through all these reports. Preaching bands of girls and teachers in this school also went out on Saturdays and Sundays as did the school boys and instructors. Teachers preached in the street gospel hall when they had no classes. Reports were given at the daily evening prayermeetings. A twelve-hour watch-tower prayer service was maintained enthusiastically in an upstairs room until school closed. The girl contributed liberally of their limited funds to work of the B.Y.P.U. societies. Fifteen were baptized this spring. This summer the graduates and other students will teach Vacation Bible Schools preach to the women in the villages, and lead prayermeetings, as will many of the boys who have gone home, for there is now a prayer-meeting nearly every night in each of the many revived country churches. This report, as did so many others, closes with words of praise: "Bless the Lord, O my soul, and all that is within me bless His holy name!"

This letter is being written at Hwanghsien, Shantung, where we are attending the Chinese Summer Bible Conference. We never saw such rejoicing as among this large body of delegates, who have come from as far north as Harbin, Manchuria, and Tsining in the far west of Shantung; nor have we ever seen the Chinese so burdened for the souls of their people. Surely with God thus blessing the work of your missionaries in such a marvelous way, when we are needed so much to direct in this movement and to teach His Word, and with unparalleled opportunity for preaching the gospel, you will not allow our forces to be cut down, or funds to be reduced, but make it possible for us to continue to GO FORWARD in the Lord and the power of His might.

Hwanghsien, Shantung, China, July 10, 1932.

C. A. L.

INCIDENTS OF THE REVIVAL IN THE CHINESE BAPTIST
CHURCHES OF THE NORTH CHINA MISSION.

III.

Chefoo, Shantung, China, July 15, 1932.

DEAR BROTHER PASTOR, BRETHERN AND SISTERS:

You who pray for the work out here and contribute of your funds for saving of the Chinese will be interested to receive another letter giving a few incidents in this great revival movement, where God is blessing so many. Please accept this as a personal letter from the one whose name the envelope bears, and pray that the revival will not only spread throughout China, but that God will also revive His people in the homeland and increase their interest in foreign missions.

In the densely populated county of Pingtu, Shantung, where the revival began and the churches have been greatly revived, there are now villages in which every family has one or more saved persons, and in some villages nearly every one has accepted the Lord. Is this not glorious news to all who love God our Savior!?!? Even during wheat harvest meetings went right on. Some coming into the meetings at night fell asleep from sheer exhaustion, desiring rather to pray than to rest.

At one of these villages a missionary dared not sleep a few years ago, for the bandits were expected at attack at any time, which meant looting and burning of the village and possible carrying away of missionary and leading Chinese for ransom or death. But since the revival began that whole community is different. Recently this same missionary slept there safely with doors open and walls down. One could not ask for more peace than now reigns in that region. Forty odd were baptized in the village this spring.

Another story is told of a gospel tent which was not being used for lack of funds and workers, now repaired and being used by laymen in Pingtu county, as at Tsinan. An organized band of desperate robbers planned to break up the meetings and take the tent. The brethren were advised to move elsewhere in order to save the tent, but replied, "No," preferring to pray earnestly for salvation of these robbers. The result was that the young bandit leader was stricken blind and a swelling came upon his face. This frightened him greatly. He realized it was from the Lord, and came to the tent confessing his sins and asking for prayer. Converted, his sight was restored and the swelling left. Later he went to Pingtu city and joined a Bible class. His life has been wonderfully transformed. This man had heard gospel in a Christian day school when a child, but resisted and has served the devil rather than God. Those who know hi believe that now he will give the remainder of his life to preaching. There have been between two and three thousand conversions in Pingtu county this year. No less than one thousand have been baptized!

At another village God's Spirit seemed to fall upon the people like fire. They fell before Him, asking for forgiveness and salvation. During a meeting the speaker arose from prayer only to see his congregation leaving the house. He found that old Sister Kiao, who had been sick was carried to the meeting, had gotten up, walked out, and was on her way home, third of a mile away, to tell her family she was healed. The village people marvel, for she had not walked for twenty years and was known to be helpless. She is still walking, and, with others, is praising God. The church is now too small, so at night two separate meetings are held.

A Christian son of a Pingtu woman who was healed clerks in a store in Tsingtau. He went home to see his mother and to rejoice with her. Seeing her, a revived church, and the salvation of many of his people, he also reconsecrated his life to the Lord. On returning to the big port city persuaded his employer to let him go out to witness for the Lord. The very first night he happened to go into a prayermeeting where someone was telling of the healing of his mother, but the leader was not sure that this and other reports of healing were true. The young man was quickly on his feet to testify to the healing power of his Lord, and preached Christ to those who had come. He continues to witness for Christ with that zeal which has taken possession of so many. The husband of this same Christian woman, who has been healed after 18 years of helplessness, lives here in Chefoo, where we are writing at this time. His family telegraphed him and he immediately went to his home, some distance interior, to see his wife and to praise God. He, too, has reconsecrated his life to the Lord, is preaching His Word, and many of his village are being saved.

It rejoices one to hear also of how God is now graciously and marvelously blessing His work in the Laichowfu field. We were permitted to labor there before moving to Harbin. A man who went home from up our way and was converted in the Laichowfu meetings was met by his brother in the fields with a shovel ready to fight, for they had been enemies for eight years. But the meeting turned into one of confession of sins, forgiveness and salvation of both. Then the two sisters also became Christians. This prodigal brother from Manchuria is now so enthusiastic in preaching that many of the heathen think him crazy.

At one of the women's prayermeetings in a neighbor's yard a missionary saw mud on the skirts of some of the women, due entirely to tears wept for sin and unsaved members of their families. A phonograph is no longer needed there to attract people into the evangelistic meetings, for the gospel hall fills with earnest listeners. Again we find the laymen there preaching in tent and other meetings, while the missionary and evangelists are free to give their time largely to work elsewhere.

In an adjoining county a leading church member who for twenty years was careless about paying his debts, has now received a new Christian experience and is advertising for creditors to present old accounts, and his son is now supporting two evangelists. A Christian man at Hwanghsien brought forward $500.00 of tithes due the Lord since he became a Christian years ago. Another who owed money to a missionary now in America but did not intend paying it has sent the money to him. Others are making restitution and paying back tithes due the Lord.

Time would fail us to tell of the many evidences of God's wonderful working in the Chinese churches. This is given that you may rejoice with us and give praise to God. The revival is a result of earnest prayer, preaching and Bible teaching. Again may we ask that you join us in prayer for return of the missionaries now at home. We plead with all earnestness for greater financial support so the saving gospel of our Lord may be carried to other places here in Shantung, in Manchuria and elsewhere, for we have never had such openings for preaching the Word as at this time.

C. A. L.

CHAPTER THREE

LIVING WATERS

"Then Peter said unto them, Repent, and be baptized every one of you in the Name of Jesus Christ for the remission of sins, and ye shall receive the gift of the Holy Ghost." Acts 2:38.

Why such good reports at the 1932 Mission Meeting as recorded in the preceding chapter? Let us look back to the Mission Meeting of 1930 in Chefoo. At that time three evangelists made discouraged reports of work among "dead" churches. There was a note of despair and hunger in the reports. Some missionaries spent the summer in seeking new spiritual light and life. At the 1931 Mission Meeting there was still more definite confession of need in spiritual power. One missionary spent the summer searching the Scriptures for teaching on the work of the Holy Spirit, going through the Old and New Testaments, and seeking light from the Greek New Testament.

Early that fall a missionary began teaching the Acts of the Apostles to a High School Class, with special stress on the Person and Power of the Holy Spirit in Kingdom work of soul winning,—the chief result being that the teacher herself became acutely conscious of her own lack of power, and the need of the Holy Spirit in fullness in her own life. News went around the Mission that one of our most true and tried missionaries had received the baptism in the Holy Spirit. That made the rest of us sick of our wilderness wanderings and anxious to cross over Jordan.

To make a long story short, from September, 1931 to June 1932, at least twenty-four missionaries and many Chinese leaders had had a definite experience of the baptism in the Holy Spirit, and were rejoicing all through the year as they saw new light and life coming into the churches. The summary in the three letters is but a meager account of what happened during the year. But let us hear from some of the missionaries themselves, informally, just as letters were passed from friend to friend during the year.

Laichow, Shantung, January 1, 1932.

DEAR BROTHER JOHN:

"Bless the Lord, O my soul; and all that is within me, bless His Holy Name."

How we do praise the Lord for His many blessings poured out upon us during the past year; and , as we look forward to the New year, we are full of thanksgiving for victories yet to be won by our blessed Redeemer. Praise His Holy Name!

God has most marvelously dealt with us during the past several weeks. On December 2nd we began a revival at Laiyang City, which lasted for nine days. From the very first, the spirit was good, and the spiritual fervor rose from day to day. Our people felt that there were spiritual blessings which they had as yet not received, and there was a deep spiritual hunger. I felt that I had lost much of my spiritual power during my twelve years in China. A you recall, I mentioned having had a deep spiritual experience twenty years ago. I felt, while at Laiyang, that it was absolutely necessary for me to get down before God in sackcloth and ashes; and it was also necessary to confess actual sins which I had winked at before.

On the evening of December 3rd we had a prayer service in the church. At first there was singing and praying in chorus. Then there was a lull, and a complete hush possessed the room. There were several of us kneeling in the front of the church. Mr. Li, our evangelist, had been suffering with hoarseness, and could hardly speak. After quite a period of stillness he began to sing a song. His voice had absolutely no huskiness in it. I realized that it was something extraordinary, and I suddenly cried out, "The Holy Spirit has come!" in Chinese. The next moment both he and I were hurled down on the floor and could not get up for about two hours. Oh! the rapture and the ecstasy of it! It seemed that I was so full that I would burst, and the fire of the Holy Spirit seemed to be burning away everything but the very purest and holiest of impulses. That night there were several who had not surrendered to Jesus, who fell down before Him and were gloriously saved. Praise His Holy Name!

Thus began one of the most glorious revivals I have ever been in, either in America or in China. Tens upon tens of people were convicted, and twenty-odd were really and truly converted, born again, in the truest sense of the word. At times I did not even get to preach, as we took up the whole preaching time dealing with souls who were crying out to God for mercy. Once I did not get to the end of my discourse before souls were crying out to God, and in agony for their sins. I wish you could have been there. It was marvelous to see how the Holy Spirit worked. Man's feeble efforts were thrust aside, and we had the privilege of standing at the side and seeing the Spirit work. Praise His Holy Name.

After returning to Laichow I rested a day, and then began an eleven day revival here. It took longer for the spiritual temperature to rise, but as the days progressed the Holy Spirit was given more freedom, and there were a goodly number born again; and Mrs. Chang Ai Chen was baptized with the Spirit. A good many of our dear people are longing for a deeper walk with God. Thank the dear Lord! I am sure that He has shown us that the greatest need in all of our churches is a full surrender and consecration of both missionaries and Chinese to the Lord Jesus Christ."

Hwanghsien, Shantung, February 10. 1932.

DEAREST LOVED ONES:

Marvelous is the Lord and wonderful are His mighty words. Praise His Name, Who is "the same yesterday, today and forever." We have had such a revival during the past week as I have never seen in my life. Such confession of sin!—till my ears and heart hurt as I thought of them. My own heart was deeply convicted and I was brought so low till I was in despair except for the blessed hope in Christ. He gave me a beautiful verse, fitting for the condition I was in Sunday morning, Isa. 54:8, and now, thank His Holy Name, I've tasted His everlasting kindness. Then during the day there were other sweet experiences, as I knew He had been "tempted in all points like as we, yet without sin," then that none of us could be "justified by the law," and then finally I realized my own helplessness in such a way that I could not live without Him. Manifestations were given me, but I cried, "O, Lord, I don't want manifestations, I want Thee," and in a few moments I was on my feet giving testimony. I began: "Who can lay anything to the charge of God's elect?" and burst out so in praise to God that I knew that the Power in me was from above, and my heart was filled with holy laughter and praise Ps. 126:2. Many other have received this blessing, some not in full, some more fully; three of our girl nurses, many of the missionaries, some servants, some evangelists,—some old, some young, some men, some women. Mr. Kiang Feng Nan, who at the beginning of the meetings said if he began confessing his sins it would take the whole time of the meeting, is now filled with the Spirit of God, and Dr. Chu, his wife and mother, five or six of the missionaries, and I can't begin to tell all the names. The Lord will soon be here. He is thrusting forth laborers into His harvest. "Ye shall receive power after that the Holy Ghost is come upon you, and ye shall be my witnesses."

Oh, beloved, turn your eyes quickly to the Lord, He has forgiven; full salvation is yours if you will rest in Him. Nothing can separate between us and God but our own sins. He is willing to remove this awful load and to hold us so tenderly that we may rest in His arms. What have we to fear if we've trusted all to Him! Oh what a miserable life is that of Romans 7, but what glorious freedom in Romans 8! Many times the meeting would last day and night, with intermission of only an hour more or less between. Every night some prayed all night. We were hungry, and God filled us. He said, "Open your mouth wide and I will fill it." Eating and sleeping were quite secondary. Sometimes Mr. ——— did not get a chance to give any message at all. He just prayed and praised God as he stood by and saw God working. Oh, read and believe God's word. Every word is true. Praise His Name! He has the same blessing for every one of you. You can't afford to live without it, and to die without it would be like the five virgins with no oil in their lamps. He is not limited to China. I pray that He give you hungry hearts that He may fill you.

A heart full of love to you all. The glory is all of Him. "Buried. . . .and hid with Christ in God." Hallelujah! Oh, the blessedness of "leaning on the Everlasting Arms." The same blessing is for you. Acts 2:39.

A WITNESS TO THE ABOUNDING GRACE OF GOD

I came to China in 1923, and for several years did my best to learn the language and witness the best I could for the Lord. I continually felt that I was powerless, and the millions of unsaved all around made me feel helpless. In 1927, while most of the missionaries were refugeeing in Chefoo, I had a conference with Miss . . . and she asked me if I had been filled with the Holy spirit. Her question puzzled me, as I had never heard a question like that and put so straightforward. But that question set me to thinking, praying and searching the Scriptures. During that time I had to face and settle many sins in my life that had come in since I had become a Christian. Great conviction came upon me, and I had to write many letters and make restitution in many cases. I got great peace and joy and my Bible became a new book. While in prayer alone at Laichow a few weeks later I asked the Lord to give ma the Fullness of the Holy Spirit. After two or three hours of prayer and meditation He gave me a most blessed experience, and I am sure now that if I had gone on with Him in that close fellowship that He would have given me what I was in so much need of. For several months I was a different person and have been in a way since that time, in that I realized as never before that God wants to fill us and possess us fully in the person of His Holy Spirit, a thing that I have not realized in the same way before. However, at that time the "Baptism of the Holy Spirit," the "Fullness of the Holy Spirit," etc. was not discussed by many people, and I just let this most wonderful experience gradually fade out, a thing that is so easily done in the busy routine on the Mission field.

In 1931 God began to work mightily in Shantung, and we were hearing of such definite workings of the Holy Spirit. I immediately remembered the blessed experience of a few years before, and a great hunger came into my soul for the renewal of that spirit and a deeper experience with the Lord. Soon I found that many, many, both Chinese and missionaries here in Hwanghsien and in other places were hungering for the same thing, and in many places that hunger was being fully satisfied.

The Holy Spirit was working mightily in Pingtu and other places, and we heard of most glorious work, which greatly increased our hunger. At the winter vacation I made a visit to Pingtu and saw and heard things that opened my heart and soul to fully realize that the wonders, miracles, and power of New Testament days had not passed away. When I returned to Hwanghsien, Mr. . . . came for a few days of witnessing. He had just been graciously blessed of the Lord, and a large group of missionaries and Chinese workers met daily to hear the testimony. In prayer I had great freedom and full assurance that God was going to bless me and others. About the second day that freedom in my prayer stopped and heaven seemed to be closed. I sat up until twelve o'clock that night to trying to pray, read my Bible and think what was the matter. Suddenly great conviction of sin came upon me, and I realized that I must fully face myself and make things right. I called my wife and made some confessions to her, and we prayed together and I got great peace.

The next morning, before Church service, in reading my Bible, the Lord used Romans 2:16-30 to show me how I had been living in trying to lead others when I had not really been taught myself. He also showed me how I had been living in trying to lead others when I had not really been taught myself. He also showed me that I should make a full confession to the group that morning, a thing that was very hard to do, but I had come to the place through the grace of God that I was willing to pay the price. When we went into the service Mr. . . .called on me for prayer, and it seemed that the Lord was never so near to me as then. When I got through praying I asked permission to make my statement. When I was through the greatest peace that I have ever felt came over me. God used my testimony to break down others, and that meeting just turned into a mutual confession of sins meeting. For days and days to come I have never seen or heard of such conviction of sin. The Spirit was no respecter of persons; no missionary escaped, no leader or worker among the Chinese escaped; old and young alike, rich and poor, were the same. For three days after I made my confession I just sat there in the meetings sometimes as long as eight and ten hours a day and praised the Lord for His mercies. My whole being seemed to be going through a great change. It seemed like a strong electric current was going through my body. The second day sitting in the meeting I saw the real meaning of Romans 8:26-27. It seemed that the Spirit was praying within me with groanings that could not be uttered. Sometimes I felt like I would die for joy, at others I would be crushed under the burden of prayer. Several times in prayer in private with Mr. . . . . it seemed to me that both of us would lose ourselves in God, but I would in my desire not to let the flesh enter into anything, shrink back from a complete surrender to God.

Finally on the fifth night of the meeting after we had dismissed, a group of four or five of us men came to my study to pray. We were praying about twelve o'clock and the Spirit came in mighty power. I had hitherto been so afraid of the flesh and evil spirits that I was afraid to really surrender to the Lord. All of a sudden Luke 11:11-13 came to me and I realized that I was God's own child and there I was right in His presence and I definitely and unreservedly surrendered my whole being right into His hands. I was fully conscious of everything and it seemed that He literally took me into His arms. I was absolutely unafraid and conscious that it was God's Holy Spirit's work. He took right hold of me and shook me (physically) as I would shake a rag, then He opened my mouth so wide that my jaw bones seemed like they would break, and the room was filled with wind and it literally rushed into me until I felt that I would burst. This happened four or five times. Then a great burst of joyous laughter that was different from any laughter that I had ever experienced, came right from deep down inside me. This happened over and over.

Next I was brought face to face with several problems that I had been thinking of those days. It seemed that the Lord Himself was asking me one by one about these problems and I would answer back "I will surrender it all to you." I answered them sometimes in English and sometimes in Chinese, all of which I was conscious of, and those in the room heard. Then it seemed that there were magnets all around me pulling everything in me out. I realized that the Lord was cleansing me, and I was saying "All gone." After that for ten or fifteen minutes I was resting, it seemed to me in the very arms of Jesus. It came to me all of a sudden that I was praying for the Fullness of the Holy Spirit and I had gotten Jesus. I was literally lost in Him and He in me. As definitely as I have every communed with any earthly friend I communed with my Lord. Suddenly a great feeling of unworthiness came over me "A poor wretched sinner in the arms of a loving Saviour." I understood this as never before, "Abounding grace." Then there came a great burden of prayer over me, and it seemed the whole world was upon my heart. After praying a while I committed it all to the Lord with the greatest assurance that He had heard my prayer. There came such peace and joy, and again we were all praying together. The Spirit continued to work until all three of us had been greatly blessed.

For those days my wife and I had been praying together and longing for the same blessing. She had become greatly discouraged and the old Adversary was accusing her terribly. For a half day such a burden for her came over me that it seemed at times my physical body could not stand it and I could not utter my prayer, but again the Spirit within me was praying. Finally the Lord took the burden and I through His faith just gave it to Him with the perfect knowledge He had heard my cry. That night my wife got a blessing and I seemed to be right in heaven praising God and love for the whole world seemed to flood my soul.

The following weeks we were abundantly blessed and we saw hundreds brought under conviction for sin and filled with joy of sins forgiven. The 32nd Psalm had more meaning that I had ever seen before. Nineteen Thirty Two has been the greatest year of my life. I have not done what I should, being so greatly blessed, but I have seen more sinners stricken under the power of the Holy Spirit than I have seen in all my life together before. "Praise the Lord, oh my soul, and all that is within me praise His Holy Name."

How Christ Dealt With Me

Never did any missionary go to a foreign land with a more shallow experience in Christ than mine. I had realized that I was not fit to come, yet did not seem to know how to become fit. People seemed to think if one was willing to go to a heathen land, then the depth of consecration and the heights of devotion had been reached.

After being in China a little while I knew I was simply against a stone wall and no power in myself to scale it, nor did I know how to lay hold on Him for the power. I was happy with my surroundings and had great joy in my home and children, but the unrest and hunger in my soul deepened. But in 1927 a book fell into my hands that made me see that my need was the Fullness of the Holy Spirit. I started praying for it. I was greatly blessed that year in many ways. In fact my prayer life was so greatly changed and my Bible became so new to me and so much changed that I thought I had had the fullness.

When we returned to China in 1930 I realized that I still was not a vessel the Lord could use, and began praying very definitely. He heard this prayer and answered it far differently from anything I had expected. The great revival had started in our province and in one of our own stations. I knew the Christians were getting what I had longed for, so my prayer efforts were greatly increased. How I do thank God that He hears us when we do not know what to pray for.

In February Mr. . . . .came to us. He had been baptized with the Spirit and was on fire. He stayed in our home. He spent much time fasting and praying during the first days of the meetings. I had been so hungry and so in earnest and felt so willing to follow the Lord. But suddenly the Lord asked me to travel a very hard, trying road. He showed me many things in my life from childhood up to that very week that I must put straight, and I was staggered, while I held back, unwilling and miserable. Then it seemed He said to me "Aren't you willing to walk for a while this road you so thoroughly deserve to when I walked it all the way to Calvary for you and bore your awful sins?" I took off the mask I had been wearing, but I realized I hadn't fooled any one except myself. I confessed what He led me to; I wrote many letters of confession to America. All that He revealed to me to get right I did, both with Chinese, missionaries and my own family. I just thank Him for giving me the strength to do this. I could not have done it in my own strength. Then a great peace and joy began to fill my soul.

But there was still a testing time to come before He came in to dwell in the fullness. I just seemed to sink into a darkness that completely engulfed me. My desire even to pray suddenly left me. I couldn't pray. A spirit of rebellion entered my heart. I know it was Satan making a last great effort to keep his long-held territory. During this period of a few hours my husband had received the baptism, and although I had prayed and longed for him to have it, I could not rejoice with him. He was immediately burdened for me. I praise the Lord that He soon brought me back to where I could pray and look to Him. Then that night a small group met in our home to wait for His outpouring. I started praying and every question that could possibly be thought of bombarded my mind. But I just said, "Lord, I just want to surrender it all to you. You only can answer." And Oh how graciously He did take such an unworthy piece of material. My heart was filled with a joy that I did not know could be felt in this world. It was joy because I was in His presence. It was then that the praise just started pouring from my heart and lips of its own accord. In fact it could not have been kept back. A spirit of intercession started in my heart and I was just lifted out of myself, praying for others. The joy just surged through me and went over me like one wave following another. The world was a new world to me, and never had God's Word been so precious as it has since. I could never praise Him enough for His loving kindness to me. The first soul I dealt with after the experience, I was able to lead to Him. This experience was just an opening of many doors to me. It deepens and grows as I yield myself to Him, day by day. I have not always been yielded, and thereby lost a blessing, and failed to honor Him. He has shown me that He expects constant growth, yet I've often been unwilling to pay the price. But I can say from the depths of my heart, "He is the fairest of ten thousand to my soul."

Miss Hou Of Pingtu

Miss Hou is an evangelist and Bible teacher of power. She had been used in a large field in Manchuria as an evangelist and in Bible school work. The writer was associated with her in three months work in Shantung, and never have we seen a more devoted servant of the Lord. In rough country work, in cold, inconvenient quarters; up at daylight to get time for private Bible study and prayer, for the rest of the day must be given to meetings and to the village people, who crowd around all day and never give any privy. Just being near such an earnest, cleansed vessel of the Lord, made the writer desire and work toward a higher plane spiritually.

During 1931 Miss Hou came home to Pingtu, led in meetings, and then was sick unto death, the sickness due to the hardships she had gladly endured. One night it was thought that she would die, but prayer saved her. As she was convalescent in the hospital she heard that revival was in progress and that one of the missionaries had received the fullness of the Spirit. She went to her Bible with which she was already familiar above the average, and "searched the Scriptures," reading The Acts, Col., and Eph., especially, memorizing Ephesians. She became convinced that there was a fullness of the Spirit which she had not experienced and began praying for it. The expressions, "singleness of heart," "Stephen, full of faith and the Holy Spirit," and "the Lord added to the church daily such as should be saved" made her hungry to have the fullness of the Spirit promised in the Acts of the Apostles. But this did not make her slack her efforts in soul winning, and one day as she was lying on the bed doing personal work with a hard-hearted nurse, who, kneeling by her bed, was at last turning to the Cross, she, Miss Hou, was so happy she could not sleep but lay on the bed singing praises to the "slain Lamb." This testimony is given to show that this Bible teacher, Seminary graduate, had not been near a meeting, and certainly not near an "emotional " meeting but her conviction of need came while reading the Bible alone. Where she had had life in spiritual things before she now has "abundant life." Where she was used before in soul winning, prayer, and Bible teaching, she is now used in a greater and more powerful way. Acts. 1:8.

A MODERN STEPHEN

Pastor K. is one of the leading pastors of our Mission. A man of much ability he could have been successful in political world where his friends at one time tried to draw him; educated and musical, he could have enjoyed himself in many walks of life, but early he put his all on the altar and became a faithful leader in Christian circles. During the summer of 1931 he became hungry for the fullness of the Holy Spirit. He had always been a deeply spiritual man and had taken every step he knew to take spiritually. At first he was afraid that he would run into "Pentecostalism" but going to the Word he became convinced that the promise in Acts 2:38 was for him. The more he studied and prayed, the more hungry he became for the "living waters" to become his experimentally. Then he went through a period of doubting, but the promise in Gal. 3:14 came to him, and he became so hungry that one night he prayed all night long. Then he became afraid of psychological influence and mesmerism, but continued to wait upon the Lord till one day while kneeling in church the Holy Spirit came into his spirit in such power that he knew the promise of "living waters" had been experimentally fulfilled. He had great joy and praised the Lord for days. Where he was a good pastor before he has now become a power in prayer and soul winning. He has the courage to go into the political circles and all walks of life for direct drives in soul winning. His church is seeing souls saved daily. He has become a modern Stephen "full of faith and of the Holy Spirit."

For fear my reader should take doctrinal exception to the term "Back to Pentecost" let us notice that we are not going back to before Pentecost, but only waiting upon the Lord to prepare our hearts to RECEIVE what He has so graciously given. We believe that the Holy Spirit came at the Pentecost, but very few believers have experimentally received Him in His fullness. Acts 6:3-5. We do not believe in "tarrying," but in "receiving"—and some of the all-night prayer meetings mentioned were not in the sense of waiting for Pentecost, but in waiting upon God for His preparation of hearts to receive what He had already given. The long prayer meetings were only an expression of the hunger of hearts for the fullness of the Spirit and not any dependence upon the length of prayers. The people were so hungry that time became as nothing to them.

CHAPTER FOUR

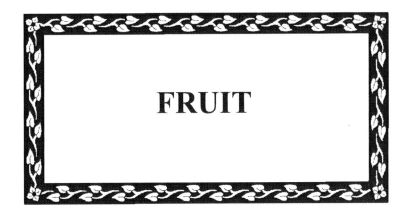

FRUIT

Two Atheists Saved

The miracles I am about to relate will not be believed by some of you at first. I did not want to believe my own eyes when I first saw it, but a year later, after checking up succeeding events, it is time to publish the facts to the praise and glory of our Lord, Jesus Christ. Mrs. Loa belonged to a church near Pingtu which was as dead, but during a remarkable revival came to life. Mrs. Loa, herself, had been a paralytic for eighteen years. Since her husband had taught in the Mission school at one time, and as she was a church member, and as the evidence is unmistakable, there is no need to go into the details of the fact that she had been unable to walk for eighteen years. During the revival at her own church, she was prayed for twice, her faith was strengthened, and she felt better. About a month later she was brought to Pingtu, and on December 10, 1931 was prayed for according to James 5. She arose immediately and walked from the missionary's home where the prayer took place over to the church, and has been walking ever since. A telegram was sent to her husband in Chefoo, but he could not believe the good news, thought that it must be mesmerism. He had spent much money on a cure for his wife, and had been told by one foreign doctor and two Chinese doctors, both graduates of foreign mission hospitals of repute, that there was no cure for his wife. He, himself knew that his wife's lower limbs were drawn up, large at the joints, but small as little sticks with no muscles at all. Nevertheless the husband put aside his work and came home doubting, but what was his joy to be met at the gate by his wife who had walked out to meet him. Then there took place the greatest miracle of all and that the softening of the heart of the husband who had forgotten God. Although in his younger years he had known the Gospel, he had put it all aside for worldly ambition, had served as an official in R.R. management; he had not been to church for ten or fifteen years, had not read his Bible in twenty years, but after seeing his wife he repented, resigned his regular work and has given his days to the spreading of the Gospel.

He loves pioneer work, and in about six months has visited eighty villages telling the Glad News in places where the people have never heard. He walks and stops to preach to the farmers as he meets them in the fields. He asks them three questions, "Do you believe in God? Do you believe you have a soul? Do you believe you have sin?" If they believe in any one of the questions then he has a point of contact to tell them of the Saviour. A brain that was once given over to doubt and political schemes is now turned to service in saving the simple farmer folk.

Another miracle took place in the family when the younger son came home to make sport of the revival which was going on in his home church. He said that from what he had heard it must be better than the picture shows he had seen in the port city where he worked. After a day or two of listening to what the Bible teaches about sin, he came under such deep conviction that he was unable to speak, was thrown to the ground in agony but got up and by gesture confessed his sins, pointing to the sins written on the poster of the black and red hearts. He was saved and went back to his work in the port city where his fellow workmen persecuted him by hiding his Bible which he loved to read daily, but he never lost patience and after his fellow workmen saw how he was able to find his Bible after prayer each time, they acknowledged the True God.

There was also another heart miracle in connection with the healing of Mrs. Loa. There is a doctor in Pingtu, one of the first graduates of a renowned missionary hospital. As an army doctor he had gone to the depths of sin such as is only possible in a land like China. Although he also had known the Gospel he left it completely and with other members of a political party had taken public oath that he would never have anything to do with Jesus or His religion. But during the revival in Pingtu he said in a scornful way that the day two of his patients, the eighteen year paralytic and another of twenty-eight years standing, walked, he would believe. By faith in prayer both rose and walked, and the doctor has repented. He has found the cleansing blood of Jesus sufficient for the depth of sin into which he had sunk.

Now he is supporting an evangelist in his home village and doing personal work among his old companions in the political party.

Praise the Lord! Hallelujah! There was not one miracle but several. Praise the Lord for the faith of His Chinese children. Praise our Heavenly Father that He is answering prayer and sending forth laborers into His harvest.

Mr. Chiang's Testimony

Mr. Chiang was a graduate of the Pingtu Mission school and after acting for sometime as evangelist, he taught in the school. Later when truly converted he admitted that he had not been happy as an evangelist, because his conscience smote him for receiving a salary to preach the Word which he did not really believe, so it was rather a relief to confine himself to school-teaching, for he could at least teach secular subjects with a clear conscience. Later he left Pingtu and taught for awhile in Laichow, then in Harbin, and ultimately went to Dairen where he did Y.M.C.A. work. On account of illness he was obliged to return home, and shortly after his return he attended a series of meetings. When he was asked the pointed question, "Are you born-again?", he frankly admitted he was not, but he resisted the Spirit and had lively discussions with his friends in the boys' school between meetings. Sometime later a preacher gave a series of addresses on the fullness of the Holy Spirit, and Mr. Chiang and his friend attended these, but they amused themselves when the meetings were over, making fun of the preacher and his message, and imitating some of the outward manifestations of the Spirit's working in the audience. Mr. Li, Chiang's friend, declared it was all mesmerism, and he claimed to be quite an authority on the subject. One day Mr. Li came out of the chapel acting as Mr. Chiang thought rather weirdly. Mr. Chiang thought he was mimicking again. "No, I've got the real thing this time," he said.

As Mr. Chiang watched him closely during the next day or two he had to admit that no mesmerism could account for such a vital change. Mr. Chiang felt rather lonely during the rest of the meetings for he could make no sport with Mr. Li, who spent his leisure moments in Bible reading and prayer. Shortly after the city meetings Miss —— and Mr. Hou went to his place to help the people, but during this series of meetings Mr. Chiang scarcely listened. Then it reached his ears that in the city many people, amongst them his daughter, were praying earnestly for his salvation, and at the closing meeting of the series he yielded to God and was immediately filled with the Spirit. From that time his Bible became the living Word. It was of such absorbing interest to him that he would read whole books of the Bible at one sitting, and within a few days he had read the Bible through. He was filled with a great compassion for the lost and was particularly burdened for those whom he had formerly caused to stumble. "I am a murderer," he said. "The bandits that are so dreadful here cause the death of only a few people, but I am the cause of the spiritual death of many. Now I am going the round visiting all the places where I preached before, confessing my former short-comings and presenting the Gospel. This is my first task. I am a debtor to them all, and I must discharge the debt." And wherever he goes the power of God rests upon him and sinners are broken down at the foot of the Cross.

Mr. Kiang Fang Nan has been a Christian for many years and is a rather wealthy and well-to-do man in Hwanghsien. He has had many temptations since being a Christian in that the Devil wanted him to lean on his own understanding, position, and wealth. By nature he like position in this world and just lately the devil had gotten him connected with some kind of official position in the city in which he got in badly with quite a number of people over finances and it became so serious that at one time he had to flee from the city. He realized that he had not done right in getting mixed up in worldly affairs and was seeking to get straight. He was just at this point when the revival began in January, 1932 in Hwanghsien. Great conviction came upon us all during those days and among the deepest was Mr. Kiang. For a week the Spirit worked upon him going deeper and deeper until on Monday of the second week he was broken down before the Lord, and he said he wept more tears on that one day than he ever had in all his life before. For a whole half day he just wept and confessed his sins before the Lord. That afternoon he went to the meeting and made a clean breast of the whole thing, "lost face" before the whole group and made things right with the Church and those whom he felt he had wronged. He was completely delivered and peace and joy came into his heart. That night he came to the prayer meeting that the Lord might prepare his heart for the fullness of the Spirit. There were probably twenty along with him. They prayed all night and about four o'clock in the morning one person who had lain down to rest suddenly felt the presence of the Holy Spirit in mighty power. This person soon awoke and realized the Holy Spirit in power. He gathered three or four persons together in a small group, Mr. Kiang among the number. They began praying and in about five minutes Mr. Kiang surrendered everything to the Lord and just accepted the fullness of the Lord. Great joy and floods of laughter came over him. He praised the Lord for nearly two hours. There were two or three others in the room praying. Finally Mr. Kiang stood up and began praying for the others, and all of a sudden he was thrown to the floor and praised and glorified God, and in a few minutes another one of the men was filled with the Spirit and wondrously blessed. Mr. Kiang has been holding meetings since that time without salary. The Lord is greatly using him. He went to Peiping and stirred up revival there. Although used to a good home and the best of food, he is now willing to suffer hardship. He loves the children of the Lord so much. Before he was prejudiced against the foreigners, but now there is no wall between, but "unity in the Spirit."

About Mr. Duan At Ch'i Li He Tzu

Both Saling and Ch'i Li He Tzu churches have been as if dead and come to life! Mr. Duan was indignant when asked if he were saved, and said, "Eighteen years a church member, baptized by one of the first missionaries, a graduate of the Seminary and not saved!" He was upset. He had preached several years. He opposed the crying and loud praying of the people who were in revival. The second day of some special meetings he could not sleep that night, for a voice kept saying, "Not saved, not saved!" Food became unpleasant. The next morning he confessed his sins and was saved and filled with the Spirit. He was knocked down as he confessed. There was a decided change in his life. Before in buying he had always had to get a little extra, now he only wants what is right. Before, when on the street or on the market, he had indulged in vile language of a special intelligent type. Now the "old man" is dead and he is a "new creature in Christ Jesus." His old companions in sin tried him out, cursed him, struck him, scorned him; but in humility he suffered it all. Outside people said, "he is certainly different." His own town people had said that when they saw that man different, they would listen to the Gospel. so he went to his neighbors, and out on the streets confessed his sins, and now that town has had a great revival and almost everybody has been saved.

A POLITICIAN BECOMES EVANGELIST

Chao Te San was one of the brightest mission pupils the early schools at Hwanghsien had. After leaving school his executive ability was turned to leadership in construction of Motor Roads and management of Railroads. While still nominally Christian he went the way of the world and the Shantung Revival found him a gray-haired retired business man enjoying the social life of Peiping. He had investments and political control enough to interest his clever brain. Sad to relate he had taken unto himself a concubine. But praise the Lord, his wife had kept in Christian circles and one day she persuaded him to go to a revival service. He did not like it specially and criticized the preacher. However in a later meeting he came under deep conviction, and began to clear up the wrong things in his life, and a few months later received the Risen Christ as Lord indeed in his heart. He put away his concubine, giving her support to be educated in a school, and made confession and restitution as far as possible in other details of his busy and varied life. Then he became concerned about the souls of his immediate family and old friends in business. Then began a series of travels going up and down the R. R. to find his old companions in sin that he might do direct personal work. sometimes his wife went with him and how her benign face did glow with happiness to see her prayers for her husband answered. Recently the Lord has called Chao Te San to special evangelistic work, and he is now out with a little group of called men, some of them uneducated, not able to read a word, but great men of prayer; most of them humble men with not a cent, but out on faith. But the expenses of the group are gladly supplied by Chao Te San, who now has only one joy in life and that to see souls born into the Kingdom. Oh! Hallelujah! What a Saviour! To pull a man out of the effete life of a retired business man into the active currents of a traveling evangelist, what a powerful work of the Holy Spirit!

LIVING EPISTLES

For years there have been programs in China such as "every one win one," and the "five years program," and efforts were made to "put them over." But now that ordinary Christians, and even boys and girls are being filled with the Spirit, the soul winning program goes on spontaneously. We have space to mention a few, only, of the hundreds of ordinary people who have been filled and turned to soul winning. When young Chang was saved his mother persecuted him, and at meal times told him to go into the yard and ask his Jesus for food. Later he was filled with the Spirit and became a power, he and a teacher went out to one of the villages and held meetings and there were many saved; he was just a High School student then. One day the missionary heard him in the church praying, earnestly lifting up his family one by one. His father and mother were the hardest ones; they too had found him in church praying and were too disgusted even to scold him. His father was an opium eater, and his mother had exhausted herself during twenty-five years of trying to manage him, said she had to sin, lose temper, to keep her husband in order. There was never any money for needs for it all went for opium. His sister had made a bad marriage of a widow who gambled and drank. Altogether the family was hopeless and dark with sin, but young Chang never gave up and now the whole family, father, mother, sisters, brothers, wife, and brother-in-law all saved. The mother repented in tears said, "The worst thing a person can do is to separate parents and child, and that is what I have been trying to do, separate the children of the Heavenly Father from him!" Young Chang is now in the Seminary at Hwanghsien and the parents have turned to soul winning, the family once "dead in sins, quickened together with Christ."

SEARCHING THE SCRIPTURES

Besides the individual Bible study which has greatly increased, there is a great demand for Bible Classes. In one station there is a very living group of people who cannot go to regular Bible School, but can give a few months or weeks to special study, or else as the local people do, go about their regular work of teaching, nursing, trading or whatever walk of life during the day, and attend the night classes. At present this group is led by a spirit filled young woman, Seminary graduate. Those who can study during the day, have Bible study in the mornings and go out after souls during the afternoons. Many good 'catches" have been made right in the class. One day a clerk from a local store brought some cloth for one of the pupils who invited him into the class and he was saved that day. The class is so of "one heart" that when an unsaved person comes into the class to listen, an understanding prayer goes up from each heart, and not a few have been saved right in the class. A worldly piano tuner came from a great port city to repair the Mission organs; one of the young men of the class, only recently saved himself, gave him a Bible, led him into the class, and before the repair work on the organs was finished, the man was saved, and filled with the Spirit.

And so on during the two years the drive for soul winning has gripped the ordinary people. In some cases a little child leads them. In the country a girl, saved and filled with the Spirit, saw a vision of Jesus on the Cross for her sins; she became so concerned for the souls of her parents and immediate family, some nominal Christians but not born-again, that she cried out as if her heart would break. The missionary gave her the promise of Acts 16:31, and she took it by simple faith. Within a few days her parents and immediate family were all saved.

The Revival has gripped all three hospitals. In one in particular there was early a great work of grace, all the nurses in the women's Hospital saved and filled with the Spirit. Even the scrub women went about their work beaming and singing praises to the Lord. The sick were saved daily. On a visit to this hospital the writer was inspired and convinced of the power from on high which caused an atmosphere of radiant souls freed from sin and rejoicing, as we are all told to rejoice in Ps. 145-150. "Praise ye the Lord: for it is good to sing praises unto our God; for it is pleasant; and praise is comely."

In one school, the two daughters of a Bible woman were filled with the Spirit; they and some classmates were on fire to witness to their own families, so one weekend they all walked thirty *li* to their home village. On Sunday they gave their testimonies to the Christians in the chapel. The hearers melted to tears, confessed their sins, and became so hungry that within a few weeks about thirty-four were filled with the Spirit. These in turn are on fire for souls and revival is spreading all through that countryside.

In a number of cases the servants have turned to witnessing. I one station two of the missionaries had special services for the servants. After several had been filled with the spirit one remarked, "We never thought the fullness of the Spirit was for us! We thought it was only for teachers and preachers." They all started witnessing and one sent for his family to come a long distance from the west in order to get them saved. In one school the old woman cook is filled with the Spirit and spends her days in praise and prayer, but never fails to get the meals on time. She is toothless and not pleasant to the eye, but the joy she has in the Lord has inspired others of higher station. On Saturdays she goes out with the girls to the villages witnessing. We are reminded of the household of Cornelius: Peter remarked, "Of a truth I perceive that God is no respecter of persons." —————— "While Peter yet spake—the Holy Ghost fell on all them which heard the word."

CHAPTER FIVE

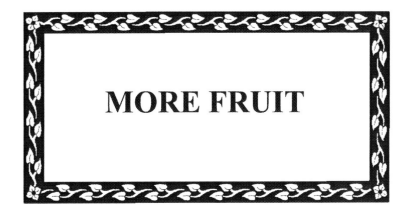

MORE FRUIT

March 24, 1932.

"He is faithful that promised." "I will sing unto the Lord, for He hath triumphed gloriously." sing forth the honour of His Name: make His praise glorious."

Last year we wrote some of you, asking you to pray that God would revive His work in Hwanghsien. And now we write to ask you to rejoice with us, for God has answered exceeding abundantly above all that we asked or thought. He has sent us a real Holy Spirit revival! Our hears are saying: "Who can utter the mighty acts of the Lord?" "Who can show forth all His praise?"

Last year we had two Chinese evangelists with us, who gave us stirring messages and we saw some souls brought in. But this year we have had the most remarkable revival in the history of this work. There has been almost no preaching, no exhorting—only prayer and the silent powerful work of the Holy Spirit. It began with the confession of sins among the missionaries and the Chinese church leaders.

A missionary from another station had, while holding a meeting in an out station, been baptized with the Holy Spirit. We invited him to come here for a few days to tell us about his experience. He was with us nine days. The telling of this experience stirred our hearts, which had long been dissatisfied with our own spiritual state and with the work we were doing. A heart searching began, and the result was that the Holy Spirit revealed to us all many things in our hearts which hindered His working through us.

The wonderful promise in Phil. 1:6 "Being confident of this very thing, that He which had begun a good work in you will perform it until the day of Jesus Christ," had been brought to our remembrance about two years ago. And He is faithful that promised. All sorts of sins were brought to light, confessed and forgiveness sought from God and man. Like the king of Ninevah, many of us "arose from his throne laid his robe from him, and covered him with sack cloth, and sat in ashes." Quarrels were made up, restitution made to God and man, and misunderstandings were healed. Truly from "the failure and disappointment of our doing He has brought miracles of His doing." We have been sitting by wondering at the miracles He has wrought.

Meetings lasted five or six hours at a time with nothing but confession of sin, one after another bringing out the hidden as well as the known sins of his life. So deep was the work that hours for eating and sleeping passed by unnoticed. And so "Judgment began at the house of God."

When sin was faithfully dealt with, and forgiveness received, many were baptized with the Holy Spirit. It is like the story in the book of Acts.

This was during the first two weeks in February. About the middle of February schools opened, and after schedules were arranged, the revival broke out in the girls' school first. Whole nights were spent in prayer and confession of sin. Over a hundred teachers and pupils were set free from sin and baptized with the Holy Spirit.

Next came the boys' school. On Sunday March 13th a Sunday school class met. upon the recital of God's work in the girls' school the power of God fell upon those boys. Before I reached the building the sound of weeping came to my ears. As I entered the room the students were on their knees crying out to God for mercy. One small boy especially attracted my attention with eyes closed, tears streaming down his face, he seemed to be in an agony of conviction for sin. Beating his hands on the seat in front of him, he said: "Lord, I am the chiefest of sinners! Forgive my sins, forgive my sins!" As sin after sin came to mind, he rose and confessed it, or called some school mate to forgiveness for injury done to him. Cases similar to this continued all morning. Many were released and then shouts of victory and joy went up to the Saviour for His great salvation. All the next morning I could hear small voices near my house singing "Hallelujah, praise the Lord."

"Hallelujah, praise the Lord" is the frequent greeting

when Christians meet each other these days.

Two children on their way to school saw the sight of something dark flying across the sky.' We'd better pray, they decided. So they knelt down in the road. A cart came along and the muleteer shouted to the children to get out of the way. They moved to one side, though not rising from their knees and continued to pray. The muleteer was filled with wonder at their behaviour and thought they were crazy. They went on to school, and when the teacher entered the room all the pupils in that room were on their knees in tears. The teacher asked them the reason for their crying. "Are you afraid?" She asked, "No, we are sinners and are weeping for our sins," they replied.

The news spread like wildfire and outsiders have been saved and baptized with the Holy Spirit.

Christians have been convicted of the sin of robbing God of the tithe, and have brought in money to pay up the tithes in arrears. One man brought six hundred and more Chinese dollars, a woman returned eighty dollars, and a poor paralytic, whose income for a year is about thirty dollars sent in over six dollars as her tithe for the two years she has been a Christian and failed to pay God His tithe.

The revival has been going on for over six weeks. Every week we have had at least one all night prayer meeting. The Holy Spirit laid on the hearts of the people a great burden for the lost, and they cried out to school mates to repent and confess their sins. These school mates came under conviction and many were saved. I sat beside one little widow in the womans' school and for a long time watched her as with tear stained face she poured out her heart to God for the lost. "Oh, Lord," she cried, "wait a year or two before coming to give these people time to repent." Then she prayed for the people all over the world. She cried in agony over the fact that they rejected the Saviour.

The most gratifying thing about it all is the zeal for lost souls which has come to all that have been blessed. Every Saturday afternoon and Sunday the students go out to be His witnesses "beginning at Jerusalem." Young and old seem to feel the responsibility of warning the unsaved that "the kingdom of heaven is at hand." I heard of a movement initiated by the students to ask for a week's holiday to go out and preach to the unsaved. A group of young girls walked ten miles to be at the Sunday service in a large market town. One was the daughter of the evangelist in that place. At the morning service these school girls got up to tell of the great work of the Holy Spirit in the girls' school here. Many of the church members broke down weeping under the burden of sin. All sorts of hidden sins were brought to light. The following Sunday when a group of workers went out to that place, they found the fallow ground already broken up. Since then we have heard that twenty-two in that town have been baptized with the Holy Spirit.

The hospital also received many blessings during these weeks. Several of the personnel received the baptism of the Holy Spirit. Among these was the cook who came one morning bringing ten dollars, saying "It is not as much as I have stolen but it is all I can pay." He was saved and several days after received the baptism of the Holy Spirit. Needless to say things have been different in the kitchen, and instead of the ugly talking we have heard so often there, it is good to hear exclamations of "Marvelous Saviour."

After the little school got its blessing, the hospital came in for a large share and nearly all of the hospital force has had this blessing. A beggar woman was brought to us nearly dead two years ago. We had little hope for her recovery for months. Her temperature going often to 105 degrees after chills indicated the trouble was not removed. After three operations and many months in bed she got well and strong. From time to time she has shown increasing interest in the Gospel. One morning she came to nurses' prayers under deep conviction and confessed to having stolen several flour sacks, five cakes of soap and a bottle of bean milk. Later in the day she brought money to pay for these things. I failed to say that after she got well she became our gatekeeper, so has been with us all this time. During these days she has had a wonderful experience of salvation and is loud in her praises of the Saviour. One of the servants, whom we felt to be such a crooked person was greatly revived and baptized with the Spirit. He told me not to allow him any salary next month since he owed the hospital that much. I heard him try to tell the gate woman about his blessing, but all he could say was "Tsai Ta Sao" (her name) "Hallelujah"! Since then I also heard him urging another worker to pray earnestly, and he ended with the exclamation "He is a wonderful Saviour"!

The enthusiasm among the boy nurses is especially lovely. All these boys with the exception of a probationer who had not previously heard the Gospel, have received the blessing and are rejoicing in the Lord. One boy for whom I had nearly given up hope came to the hospital the other day. He has recently finished training and set up a medicine shop nearby. He came expecting the nurses to ask him about his business, but one by one they asked him about the condition of his heart until he was quite overcome. In making rounds I found him in the ward and asked him a similar question, we invited him to stay for our chapel. After prayers he began to tell me of a confession he should make to one of the girl nurses. We called her but as we waited, he took his hat and began ripping out the lining. I said nothing though I wondered why he was doing such a thing. "This is yours," he said, handing me the lining which proved to be one of the patient's caps. He is too far away to come to our nurses' meetings, but we are remembering him as he goes about making things right with man and God.

The sewing woman who was in deep distress about her home conditions, which were very bad indeed, is now happy in the Lord. She is spending what time she has to learn to read the Bible.

As in the schools so in the hospital there is a Spirit of concern for the lost. On last Saturday, one boy who had an afternoon off duty went home. He had been up much at night praying and was tired. He lay down and slept. When he woke up he was very much put out with himself for such a lack of zeal, and that night when he came to the meeting bringing a boy with him to hear the Gospel, he made a very humble confession of his wrong doing. He said "To think, I have been so lazy to spend my time sleeping, when there are souls being lost." Time would fail me to tell of all of God's wonderful works in our midst. We may express it in the words of the favorite verse of one of our nurses "O clap your hands, all ye people; shout unto God with the voice of triumph."

We believe that we shall yet see the walls of Hwanghsien city fall down, and Jesus riding in triumph through its streets. Praise His Name. "Come let us exalt His name together."

The Shantung revival has penetrated into high official groups. A Harvard graduate high up in government affairs was called to face eternal questions by the tragic death of a small son; a missionary surgeon went to him in sympathy but at the same time asked him to face the question of sin in his own life. He was gloriously converted and immediately turned to Bible study and to personal work. He now has a

Bible study group with his large office force, and family prayers daily in his home. His wife is the daughter of a famous evangelist and a Mount Holyoke graduate, but only recently came into a experimental knowledge of Jesus Christ as Savior. Now both husband and wife are happy in the Lord and are being used as living epistles. The man recently upset the regime of officialdom by refusing to take charge of the government lottery for improvement of roads, et cetera. The appointment had already been made and of course it meant thousands of dollars legalized personal gain, and on the face of it seemed such a good thing for the country, but a Christian conscience had been awakened, so he turned it down flat, giving his reasons. He was threatened with dismissal, but is still holding his position, and only eager to go forward in his Christian life. And so a born-again experience is making its imprint in government circles.

The revival has also gone into University circles and many college students have been saved. We cannot take space for more than one example of how the Spirit is changing young lives in college circles. Mr. Yang, the student in question, had been the head of an evangelistic band of the old formal type, and had given it up because he felt that it was all a "hull" of a nut with no life or "kernel" at the center. But ambitious and energetic he decided to prepare himself to be an educational leader, and immediately made good in college circles, and became very popular with his fellow students because he won the first place in discus throw in an all China athletic meet. He was then faced with the problem of leading the popular life of an athlete. A government college immediately offered him free tuition just for the privilege of having him as their student, but he was becoming interested in the revival, and was wise enough to remain where he could get the better educational advantage. Later he was born again, and immediately turned to soul winning by personal work; then he became anxious for the fullness of the Holy Spirit in his life and did not rest satisfied till he experienced the "living waters" promised in Jno. 7:38,39. He is now a zealous soul winner; and his powers and energies are finding new outlets. Boys come to him to learn how the discus throw is done and he gladly tells them and then turns the occasion to account by telling them of the Saviour. Recently a burden was on his heart for his home village and for his father who was sick. So he took a special occasion to return home, not only for his father's sake but in hopes of seeing a revival in the local church which was "dead". He came back rejoicing and praising the work of the Holy Spirit which has touched the whole village to the confessing of sins, tearing down of idols, making up of quarrels, and changing rough village boys into children who had experienced the power of the cleansing of the Blood; and instead of spending their days in fights and vile talk were praising a Lord who had saved them. This is only one case of many where the revival in college circles has worked back into the home life. This of course has always been the ideal but it never worked before.

The following letter was written by a missionary who has been on her country field for months at a time this winter. Only those who understand the strain and hardships of camping out on country fields can understand what a miracle has been wrought in that she not only had spiritual strength, but physical strength also. The letter shows how the promise in Josh. 1:3 was fulfilled:

LATER FRUITS

Pingtu, Shantung, China,
January, 1933.

"My Dear Friends:

Again will you let me tell some of the wonderful things that He was wrought in our midst. How we do praise Him for these months of revival, and still the blessings flow. Praise Him; Praise Him!

Different evangelistic bands have been holding meetings over the county, and also in the city. Many have been saved and many seeking to know our Saviour. The Band in which I worked is just in from a 43 days' tour. Meetings were held in churches in homes, in schools,—just any place where there was a group of Christians. We worked first with the Christians; after their hearts were right with the Lord, after they had asked for and received the infilling of the Holy Spirit, then they went out seeking their neighbors for Christ. It is easy to win the lost when His Spirit has free, clean channels through which to work.

One man had had a difference with his brother and had not spoken to him in years. He felt, of course, that he had been wronged; but after his heart was right he went weeping to his brother begging forgiveness. The brother came with him to church and was gloriously saved. He and his household were saved. It was a joyous time there in that little church, as well as with the angels in heaven.

A young girl came to me with a little bit of money and said she had stolen it from her sister-in-law and had not the face to return it, so wanted to give it to the poor, or help in some way. I begged her to take it to the rightful owner, then when she felt she hadn't the strength to do this I went with her. We had been praying for this sister-in-law and husband, and this proved to be a help in winning them to Christ. They were saved. When the differences are all out of the way then HE works.

There were some things that we did not understand, that is, had not witnessed before; people dreaming dreams and seeing visions. Before we closed the meeting one evening we were praying. Then we arose from our knees one brother said: 'Brethren, as we prayed I saw a pitchfork pass before my eyes. Is there one of our number guilty of having stolen a pitchfork?' The meeting closed quietly and all went home. But Mr. L. . . . one of the number, had a sleepless night. He spent the night trying to argue the pitchfork out with the Lord. He had stolen a pitchfork 20 years before, and that was before he became a Christian,—surely that would not count. But still he could not get rid of the pitchfork. At sunrise prayer meeting the next morning he arose and said: 'Brethren, I am the guilty party; I stole a pitchfork 20 years ago. It had left my mind until the brother saw it in a vision last night. I am guilty, but I feel that I can hardly go to this heathen neighbor and confess this sin. Pray for me.' We prayed. After breakfast he took money to his neighbor to pay for the tool, begged him to forgive him, and brought this neighbor to church to hear of the Jesus who can change people's hearts like that. Thus the gospel message entered another home.

Sometimes the vision is that Jesus is coming back, Oh! so soon, and that the people are not ready. Then there is great pleading that people repent and turn to Jesus for salvation. One little girl of twelve saw Jesus hanging on the Cross. This almost broke her heart. She arose weeping and begging for prayer for her unsaved parents. Thanks be to our Father, they were saved too. Again there was joy in heaven and on earth over sinners who repented.

There are visions of heaven and visions of hell. The Spirit uses all these in calling people to repentance.

While on this itinerary two young men teachers

came pleading that we go to their school for meetings. Mr. Chen is of a Christian family and within recent months has become very earnest. Mr. Miao is a recent convert from a heathen family. They were anxious that their fifty pupils, almost every one from heathen homes, be saved. The Spirit worked mightily in these meetings; every one of the pupils was saved. These boys were filled with a consuming desire to see others saved. They were to their homes some to outside towns, pleading with their parents and others to "flee the wrath to come," to come to Jesus for salvation. Many came and were saved, but some refused to have anything to do with this Jesus religion. Those who turned to Christ took down their house gods that they have worshipped through the ages, and burned them up. Now they are free and on the Jesus road. Their hearts are filled with joy and praise.

While a number of the parents of these boys were saved, yet the majority were not, so at the end of the year these two earnest young teachers were asked to resign. How our hearts ache for the young pupils without this Christian influence. Pray for them. We believe the Lord will open work for the two teachers.

At one place, because of several out of town guests attending the meetings there was no room for me in a Christian home, but a friendly old gentleman and his wife kindly gave me a room in their home. They knew something of Christianity; he had read a Gospel or so; but still they held their idol worship. The Spirit worked in their hearts. After a few days the old gentleman was under deep conviction of sin. Then he came to Jesus with his burden, and was cleansed by the precious blood of Jesus. He was so happy. And then he said, ' This will never do. We must go the same road.' He rushed home to tell his wife that he was saved, and heaven was his home, and that she must be saved too. I entered the room about that time. He turned and said, 'Tell her how to be saved. Tell her that Jesus saves . . we must go the same road.' So she, too, was born into the heavenly family. There were so happy in this new-found faith. He said: 'I am a new creature, old things have passed away. No more smoking, no more wine drinking, no more vile words to come from these lips. We two belong to Jesus. This home is His. No more paper and incense burned here, no more idol worship here. O, why have we found the true way so late in life! But I do thank Him we have found it.' He is going about seeking his friends and telling them that Jesus is the WAY. Do pray for them.

We do thank our Father that hundreds of the people have been saved, that the churches have been revived. We praise Him that in many places the people meet daily for Bible study and prayer and that many are seeking the lost for Christ. How we do need prayer help. The multitudes are still outside the fold, still bowing down to idols of wood and stone, etc. Pray for China. She is sin-sick. Pray for us.

We praise God for His mighty works among us. Souls are saved, backsliders reclaimed, churches revived, sick healed, demons cast out in His Name. Our hearts are full of praise to His great and worthy Name. People are going everywhere telling what great things the Lord has done for them. Pray for us. Praise with us."

CHAPTER SIX

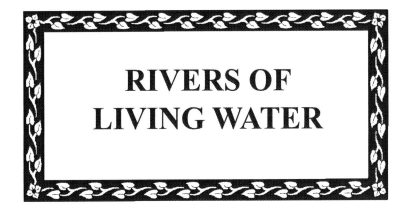

RIVERS OF
LIVING WATER

In the fall of 1932 a missionary who knew the district, was sent to inspect the work of the Revival in a mountainous section, the Home Mission work of the Native Association, with only Chinese evangelists in charge. Some of the work was so "dead" that a few years before there had been talk of closing most of it. The missionary took the trip, part of the time walking through rough mountains, in some doubt as to what he should find, but came back rejoicing that the "dry bones" had come to life. Below are a few extracts from his report:

RIVERS IN THE DESERT

About ten years ago we visited Yen Chia Chuang, when there was not only no welcome but the church doors had been sealed against our holding a meeting. On the present occasion, although we were unexpected, men and women crowded into the church to welcome us. A meeting was appointed for the following morning, and though it was a very busy season, the chapel was overcrowded with joyful workers. A communion service followed the address, and we were impressed by the sense of deep appreciation of the Cross, and the realization of the fellowship of the Lord Himself. An opportunity was given while heads were bowed for any to confess sin, and quite a few with tears poured out their sins before the Lord. For the first time we observed deep conviction on account of Sabbath breaking. Constrained by the love of Jesus Christ, men and women are going around making the Glad Tidings known in the districts around. There is no need for foreign supervision, or even of encouragement from the city church, for they cannot but tell things they have seen and heard.

Now we come to a place called Lungt'ing. About two years ago the Chinese Association thought seriously of closing this place. But here God proved Himself the God of the impossible, in calling the dead to life. Among a group of earnest worshippers are quite a few who have been baptized with the Holy Spirit. During this period of deadness two old men had continued faithful and had met Sunday after Sunday, just the two of them, for Bible reading, prayer and praise.

The third place was in a section continually raided by bandits. As in the apostolic days, dispersion has meant spread of the Gospel. The church instead of ceasing to exist has been scattered into twenty-three separate units, where worship is held every day. The evangelist lives in the fortress of refuge and goes down day by day to visit the little groups.

At one center, with the exception of the chapel and two or three homes, all the buildings had been burned to the ground. We found the people spending the nights in the fortress on the hill and going down to work in their fields by day. The fact of their position in Christ "in the heavenlies" is so real to these Christians, that despite outward desolation, they rise to greet each new day with praises and hallelujahs! Would Christ speak to them as He spoke to Smyrna of old, "I know they works, and tribulation, and poverty—but thou art rich!"?

In this same bandit section our hearts were gladdened by a dear old woman. She was only converted last spring, and at that time she could not read, but now in spite of her seventy-three years, she has learned to read, and her eyesight is better. She takes her copies of the four Gospels, the only Bible that has come into her hands, and goes everywhere preaching. One of the churches in the district, recognizing her spiritual power, have invited her to be pastor of the flock.

It could be written of the believers in the districts mention, as it was recorded of the early disciples "and they went forth and preached everywhere, the Lord working with them and confirming the Word with signs following." We saw a man who formerly had crawled around like a worm because his legs had grown together, but God responded immediately to the prayer of faith, and as these simple believers waited on Him, the flesh was torn apart, the man rose and walked, and is now going about preaching the Gospel.

We worshipped in a newly-built chapel the history of which is interesting. Several months ago an old man was dying of TB. The coffin, and even the grave clothes, were all prepared, and the people were waiting for his death. At this point the evangelist came and prayed for him, and he jumped up, calling out, "I am well!" He sold his coffin, and the proceeds were contributed towards the erection of the chapel. Several of the Christians also contributed, and the labor was by the church member themselves. At another place we were greeted by a man over seventy, who for several years had been blind, but was healed in response to the prayer of faith. At an informal testimony meeting, a fortune teller, who until recently had been an useful instrument in the hands of the Devil, related how the previous day he had been called to pray for a devil-possessed woman and in reliance on Him who was manifested to destroy the works of the Devil, the evil spirit was cast out. We saw two men who had been healed of leprosy. In one case the hands were crippled, the fingers drawn in, and the flesh of the face swollen and diseased, but healing was granted in answer to prayer.

However, throughout the district healing was not stressed, but the emphasis was on repentance and confession of sin. The proof of the reality of the revival is seen in transformed lives. Souls are being born continually through the spontaneous testimony of those who have found full salvation at the foot of the Cross. In these isolated districts God is fulfilling His promise, "Behold, I will do a new thing: now it shall spring forth; shall ye not know it? I will even make a way in the wilderness, and rivers in the desert."

Again from a letter we get a glimpse of how revival

goes into the villages on the regular fields:

"Now will you go with me to visit one of our country churches. It was spring, and the food poor, and the people busy with their crops. But the little new church, built by the Christians themselves, was full each meeting. Morning prayers started before sun up and then three other services during the day. We saw men broken down and weeping over their sins, old ladies making up village quarrels, a young boy returning money found by him, and another younger son who had made his family miserable with his hate and greed, getting free from the sins which had bound him, and the sins which he had committed as a soldier. One night Miss Liu, the young woman recently called to soul winning, rose spontaneously and started singing, "I will arise and go to my Father,"—just the Bible words. By the time she sang it twice, the whole audience were on their knees pouring out their souls to God. A demon in a woman who wanted to be saved, showed up and tried to turn the attention of the audience, but the saved and cleansed ones joined their hearts in faith, and by the power of God the demon was cast out, and the woman who was possessed has since turned to soul-winning herself.

"The revival did not close with the special meetings, but the young local evangelist and Christians have continued soul winning day by day. Never have I seen anything more beautiful than the broken spirit of the young evangelist. He wept with repentant sinners, and rejoiced with them as they received their freedom in Christ Jesus. The visiting evangelist was our own pastor Peter Wang of Hwanghsien, who had given up a "white-collar" office job down in Shanghai at a good salary to obey the voice of the Lord, and come back to Shantung to live the hard life of a traveling evangelist without salary, depending upon the Lord to supply his every need. The food which the dear country Christians provided for us was the worst either Pastor Wang or I had ever eaten, but we were so happy to see souls being born into the Kingdom that most of meal time was spent in singing and rejoicing. The most radiant of the little band was Miss Liu, only 24 years old, whose prayer every morning was to know only Christ and Him crucified. Her prayer was answered, and for the last few days she was kept busy helping repentant sinners who wanted to leave their burdens at the Cross.

"Dear reader, are you having your part in this World Revival? Won't you hunt out the promises of revival in the Bible and claim them for the World.? There is no greater force in the spiritual Kingdom than prayer. Sunday our young evangelist said, "Prayer is the blood-bought way to the Throne of Grace."

"We are truly thankful for what we have seen and heard of revival here in Shantung this year, but we are not satisfied. We want more souls saved, more of the power of the Holy Spirit in our lives and of each Christian. We want an all-China revival, to be a part of an All-World Revival. We are praying for revival in America; are you praying for us?"

"The Occidental mind starts at the very mention of dreams and visions being taken seriously, but the Oriental takes to both as naturally as the air he breathes, and much more seriously." Dreams and visions have not been the major note in this Revival but they have certainly played a part. Below we give one of the most startling examples.

"Today Mr. Hou told about the $400.00. Four pupils praying together saw the "Books"; and saw their teacher's name, not on the Book of Life but on the records of sin, and saw $400.00 that he had stolen little by little from one of our Mission schools, where he was employed and handled money. The four pupils were afraid to tell their teacher, and feared to keep it. However, they were so sad that their teacher's name was not in the Book of Life that they went to him weeping and said that they had something to say to him, but feared to say it. They were kneeling before him; the teacher begged them to tell what was in their hearts. When they told him he broke out in perspiration, and said, "I am guilty. I thought no one would every know.' He made restitution, and now God is using him as a wonderful witness."

"God is working here; souls are being saved; old scores settled; people walking out several li to speak to enemies, and bringing them to church. Several have received the Baptism of the Holy Spirit. They are seeking the lost. Oh, praise His Name! You are praying for us, I know.

December 7: Oh, praise and bless His Holy Name! He is worthy of praise! We moved today to another place, not a church,—just some cold dead church members here. We had not planned to come to this place as it is not far from the place where we had just been, but surely He sent us here. He is already working. But the other place, the one we went to from the city. Last year we tried to go there, but they were too dead to want us. That is also not a church, but a considerable number of church members. The blessed Holy Spirit just struck deep, deep, into many hearts. The church members got saved, and most of them filled."

Some of the Chinese cannot read, but they can hear and believe. The "Praying Wang" mentioned in the miracle below cannot read a word, but he has heard and believed the Word. He is a living example of what Paul mentions in I Cor. 1:27, ' But God hath chosen the foolish things of the world to confound the wise; and God hath chosen the weak things of the world to confound the things which are mighty.' But let us hear for ourselves.

THE STORY OF SAMUEL

"On Saturday, October 29th, in the village of "T'ao Yuan," a heathen father and mother were in sore distress, because they had already lost seven children, and their only remaining child, and infant of eight months, was in the grip of death. As the little body grew cold, it was transferred from the bed to the ground, and neighbors came in to comfort the parents. Some of them had heard at the Gospel Boat of One, Jesus, Who raised the dead. 'They told us there of the raising of Lazarus, who was dead four days, and your baby has only gone one hour," they said. A faint ray of hope revived in the hearts of the parents, and a messenger was dispatched to the boat 10 li away. When the workers there learned the circumstances, they brought the baby in faith to the 'God of the Impossible' and then "praying Wang" one of their number, set out for the home where the child lay. When he and the messenger arrived, the latter was surprised to find the baby lying on the bed, for when he left it had been placed on the ground; but those at home had seen a flicker of the baby's eyelids at about the time the group on the boat were praying, so they picked it up and placed it on the bed. Wang then prayed, and God was quick to respond to the prayer of faith, for before he had finished his prayer the baby cried, and great was the joy of the parents the following morning when the baby responded to their attentions by a happy smile. That day, Sunday, October 30th, the father and mother took the baby in an ox cart to the Boat, confessed their faith, gave glory to the true God, and dedicated the baby to Him."

ANNUAL REPORT OF ONE STATION FOR 1932

"Jehovah hath done great things for us, whereof we are glad."

How can one begin to tell all the wonderful things that God hath done in our midst? This has truly been one of our very best years in China. How marvelously has our dear Lord blessed us all! Both missionaries and natives have received great spiritual blessings, and the work in general has been revived.

A year ago we began revival in Laiyang City. For some time we had felt the great lack of spiritual power in our own individual as well as in the life of our churches. There was withal a great spiritual hunger in the hearts of many. At the meeting above mentioned we claimed the promise in Luke 11:13 as our own, and our precious Lord answered in a most marvelous way. Never shall we forget that night when the fire fell! The little church was transmuted into a veritable Paradise, and we were transported into the heavenly realms, and caught a glimpse of their transcendent glory and splendor. It is absolutely beyond the power of human tongue to express the sheer joy and rapture of this new, marvelous, intimate fellowship into which we were brought with the glorified Redeemer Himself. The very atmosphere of the church became electrified with power from on high. Several persons who had been under deep conviction of sin were released that night and found peace at the foot of the cross.

Glory to God! On that night began the most powerful revival ever witnessed in that little church. During the following days of meeting scores of souls came under deep conviction of sin.

Upon our return to Laichow we began a revival meeting. So wonderfully did the Holy Spirit work that the meeting was extended several days, and a goodly number of people found peace and joy in the Lord. It has been inspiring indeed to stand at the side and see the work of the Holy Spirit. We used to try to do the work ourselves, but, praise the Lord! now we are happy to let Him have the right of way. He gets all the glory, we get a great blessing, and souls are born again.

. . . . . . The power of God has been greatly manifested wherever the tent has been pitched, and many have come to scoff, but stopped to pray. . . . Never have we seen leaders and people so on fire for the Lord. Listen to the testimony of one brother:

'We used to go to church services out of a sense of duty, and when our pastor came to preach we wished for the church services to close as soon as possible, so that we might get back to our own work again. Now, however, it is different. We do not wish the meetings to come to a close, as we enjoy them so much.' It is a common thing to have a church service last for five or six hours, and then find the people unwilling to go to their homes.

One young Christian had not been on speaking terms

with his elder brother for several years. Having gotten right with the Lord, he had to go and see his brother, who, when he saw his younger brother coming, thought that surely new trouble was in store. Imagine his surprise when his younger brother suddenly 'kowtowed' to him and begged his forgiveness. He was so impressed that he readily forgave his younger brother, and also begged the latter to forgive him. The sequence? The elder brother came under deep conviction and sought the Lord for pardon and cleansing. Glory to God!

A young man was converted, and became a faithful witness of the saving power of Christ. As a result, the whole family was greatly blessed, and all but his younger brother found peace.

This past year has been worth all the others spent in China. To God be all the glory! What a wonderful joy it is to see souls born into the Kingdom.

FROM TSINGING, JANUARY 14, 1933

"A young doctor was converted last winter. He was a most promising young Christian, but his life was greatly hindered by his wife, who became violently anti-Christian. Several times she threatened to commit suicide if he went to church. If the evangelists visited in his home, she would curse them; if the Christian women called on her she was very rude to them. All were burdened for her and prayed daily for her.

At the close of one evening service, the doctor rose up and said that the Spirit had moved him to go home and confess one sin to his wife that he had never confessed to her, and asked that we pray for him. To our great delight, the wife came to the afternoon service the next day. At the close of the evening service, the doctor again rose to give a testimony. He told how he had confessed to his wife the night before, and how his confession broke down her opposition, thus showing that he had been the sinner causing her to stumble. He ended his story by telling his burning desire to see his wife saved, so they two could be of one mind and heart in Christ. With tears streaming down his cheeks and his arms uplifted in supplication to her as she sat in the balcony listening to him, he pled with her to walk down to the front of the church and kneel with him before the great throng and ask them to pray for her that she might be saved. To our great joy that timid lady came to the front and kneeled with him and all poured out our hearts to God for her salvation. Praise the Lord who hears all our petitions, she was saved before she got off her knees. We felt that another Saul had been saved, for she, too, had been a persecutor of the saints.

Revival Begins In Honan

"Sing unto Him, sing Psalms unto Him; talk ye of all His wondrous works." Psalm 105:2.

The Lord has been doing His own work here these days, for which we give our King praise, glory and honor.

Mrs. ——is one of the happiest women around, for the Lord has heard prayer for salvation of her loved ones. Since she received a blessing herself last summer, she has been praying for her sister-in-law with whom she had been 'at outs,' and for her husband. In this meeting her sister-in-law was first saved, then her niece, next her servant woman. On Tuesday she invited the evangelists and Pastor Tung for dinner. After the meal they prayed, and Mr. — confessed his sins, broke his wine bottle, and handed over his cigarette case to Pastor Chi, and found joy in the Lord. Since Mrs. —— conversion Mr. —— has persecuted her, and though he was treasurer of the church, has sneered at the idea of the new birth. Now he is different. Yesterday afternoon they both went to a village to tell the Gospel story.

Another happy family is the ——. Last April she received the Baptism of the Holy Spirit, and at that time was given a burden of prayer for her husband, an unsaved officer in the church. The Lord gave her the assurance that He was the one who turned back hearts, and she has held on to the Lord through severe trials. One time her husband grabbed her by the hair and threw her to the floor, but she praised the Lord that there was no ill-feeling in her heart toward him. He did not want her to go to church. The two little boys followed their father and they did not want to go hear the Word of God. On Wednesday, the last day of the meeting, he was invited to eat supper at the same place as the evangelists. There he confessed his sins. that night he confessed before the church, and wept like a baby. At the Sunday evening service he was present with his two boys by his side. In the afternoon he was out in the villages with a group to tell the Gospel. Pray for him that he may receive the power of the Holy Spirit and be a faithful witness among his business friends of the Lunghai Railway where he is assistant accountant.

LATER FRUITS

Laichowfu, Shanghai, January 30, 1933.

DEAR FRIENDS:

How can I ever begin to tell you of the glorious time we have had this past week at our hospitals. At the time of the Executive Committee meeting pastor Kuan of Pingtu passed through here, and I asked him to lead a service with our hospital folks. After the meeting I felt impressed to ask him to pray for me—especially for my health—and as to what the Lord would have me do, since most folks thought I should not carry on this year. I have been very much better and stronger ever since. Since then I have felt I must have him here at Laichow, and I invited him to have some meetings with our hospital folks and perhaps a few others who might be especially helped.

Well, praise His Name, Pastor Kuan came and the results have been far beyond anything I had dreamed of. I had planned two nice orderly meetings a day, and we just let HIM have His way. I can't tell numbers, but there have been some saved, sins confessed, and we think about twenty-eight who received the filling of the Holy Spirit—some few refilled—but many for the first time. Every one of our girl nurses, five of them, and our head nurse at the men's hospital, Mr. Liu, some of the helpers, including my cook, received,—some more than others. Mr. T'se Shoe E is simply beside himself with joy. I never saw anything equal to it. As Miss H. expressed it: "When he died he died all over."

There was one woman for whom I had asked prayer before the meeting began. I said as I saw her she seemed hopeless, but "all things are possible with God," and praise His Name, it is true. She was saved and gloriously filled. She is the wife of the older nurse, Mr. Kiang.

Another woman has been troubled and unhappy about her sins for a long time. She finally got perfectly straight, and she was beautifully filled. I have never seen such peace on a face. She is just about the homeliest woman

I know ordinarily, but she was lovely as she sat there with that wonderful peace on her face.

Well, I just can't begin to tell all. I have never seen anything like the way the Lord just answered prayer and the way the Spirit just took hold. Pastor Kuan is most certainly used of the Spirit. He had perfect control of things. I shall never forget how it looked as though he simply could not stand it as he listened to one young woman confess her sins, while we were all kneeling and praying. He simply sobbed out to the Lord that the Lord knew he had heard sins confessed enough, and then he just poured out his heart while she went on. After she had finished she was filled with the Spirit.

MARY C.'S EXPERIENCE

One of the noted results of the revival has been how the Spirit has worked in convicting power on people who have not been personally dealt with in regard to their salvation. One of these is Mary C. aged six. As a little child of two or three she did not like to go to Sunday School nor any kind of religious service. Bible stories did not appeal to her much—she always preferred some other kind, but nevertheless she had a Bible story almost every day. Then when she was five years old she often asked questions that showed she was thinking, and usually her questions revealed doubt. Once she said: "How can we know that God really wrote the Bible?" This had seemed to bother her much. Her mother replied: "One way we know is to read and hear it read more. Because the more one knows it, the more he knows no man could have written it." She said, "Well, we will have more Bible stories." After that we read through all the main parts of the Bible in a few months, and her interest increased steadily. In the fall of 1931 she began to be worried about her soul. She would say things at the most unexpected times about her concern for herself. This just kept on, yet neither of her parents had ever made an appeal to her to accept the Lord. They had just thought she was too young to understand. But she had heard the way of salvation explained many times.

As time went on she spoke more often of her soul. She would suddenly make a remark like this when topics of religion were not even being discussed: "How can I be saved? It just bothers me all the time to know how to keep from going to hell." Or, "Babies who die are lucky, because they all go to heaven." She said this many times. Her parents became convinced that she was under conviction, but felt it to be such a delicate thing, and she so small, that they just held back from bringing her to any kind of a decision. One night after she had gone to bed her mother read to her the story of Elisha healing Naaman. When the part about Elisha's servant was read,,—how he ran after Naaman and hold him the lies and got the money and garments, and then was covered with leprosy because of his sin, her mother saw that she was very much moved. She said, "Mary, what is the trouble?" Mary asked, "Was that servant saved?" "If he repented and confessed his sin, he was," her mother replied. Then Mary burst into tears and said "I have an awful lot of sins." Her mother, feeling so helpless, and praying silently to God, said, "Well, you do not have to keep them. Just confess them and ask Jesus to take them all away." Then she started and told her mother all kinds of things that she had done from the time she was three years old. There were all definite sins, such as telling lies, doing things on the sly that she knew were forbidden, being mean to playmates, etc. Often during this she would break down and cry. Her mother pointed her to Jesus the best she could, and tried to guide her to trust His cleansing. Her heart seemed so burdened for sin that she could not lay hold on Christ. After her mother thought she was asleep two or three times she would say, "Mamma, there is another one," and she would tell her something else on her heart. The next morning when she got up, when nothing had been mentioned of the previous evening's conversation, she said, "Mamma, there are two more things I have not told you." Both of these were untruths she had told her parents.

After this she seemed to have some peace, but both parents knew she had not yet been saved. She herself did not think so. Although no one said so to her, she told a little playmate that her heart was the black one on the poster, and not the white one. She kept making remarks that showed the Spirit was working. Finally after about three months, one day her mother was reading to her Acts 10. When she heard how these Gentiles were saved and filled with the Spirit, she just started to weep, and said, "Oh, I wish I could be saved and filled with the Spirit, so I would know I was saved." Then her mother used Luke 11:9-10, with many simple illustrations to show her to just commit her soul to Jesus. She seemed to grasp the promise and certainly peace came to her. Since then she has told many people how she was saved. She has asked many children if they are saved, and told them how she was. Her life is not faultless by any means, but she has remained sensitive to sin, and often confesses to her mother how she has sinned. Her parents have never once told her she was saved, but have always tried to show her that only the Holy Spirit could tell her that.

The above is the testimony of a small daughter of missionaries showing how the revival reached the children. Many Chinese children have been saved also.

The revival is spreading out into the country districts in a new and vital way that reminds one of the work in Samaria in the Apostolic days. Through the key of prayer of faith for sickness, doors have opened for the telling of the Glad News. In the case of a young college student who had been treated in a first class University hospital and sent home to die; confession of sin and the prayer of faith not only brought about his cure but proved to be the key which unlocked the whole district from their prejudice against the foreign religion. Several years ago one village told the preacher who came in to leave and preach Jesus somewhere else that they had determined not to receive Him. But now in this same village the simple faith of a woman recently saved in another village brought about the salvation of numbers in the village. A woman had been laid out in her burial clothes and her family were mourning for her. (In China this is done just when all hope is gone. The little blue bag of two kinds of flour, hair, and thorns had already been put up her sleeves. This prepared the for protection against the dogs as she passed through Hades. The flour to be eaten by the dogs, and the thorns to stick them. Just as the family were mourning, the woman's eyes closed, a woman who had been saved only a few days came in and said, "Oh! you must pray to the Living God; He hears prayers." She prayed and the woman opened her eyes and immediately became better. Then the believing woman witnessed to the power of the Gospel to the Salvation of souls; sent for an old man experienced in prayer, and the family themselves sent for the missionary and her co-worker. There followed the salvation of the whole family and numbers of others. About twenty in the village were filled with the Spirit. So the work goes, starting in some center and radiating out into all directions. From the record of the work of the Holy Spirit in the hearts of men is not this what we should all look forward to and expect in the present Dispensation? The saved and filled people are now singing Rev. 7:12, and other Scriptures which give the glory to God.

Another marked witness to the depth of the revival is the difference it has made in Communion services. I have heard this from not one missionary but many. Recently the Lord's Supper in the revived churches brings about a season of the memorial of the Cross and what it means in man's relation to God that is most too sacred to try to describe. One young widow told me, "My eyes were streaming tears, it was simply that I was broken before the Lord." In some cases sins are confessed before taking the cup which show a new consciousness of the exceeding sinfulness of sin, sins such as Sabbath breaking. A new sense of the holiness of God, and the necessity for pure hearts "as He is pure." One missionary remarked, "I had never been so blessed in my life as when taking communion with Spirit filled Chinese brothers and sisters in Christ."

There has been opposition from some missionaries because of lack of understanding, because the church had not kept in its old safe and sound ruts, where nothing ever happened except that the church members grew cold, went back to their old habits of drinking and smoking opium, and in the case of the women back to idol worship. The most telling and sure evidence of changed lives; opium given up, idols torn down, quarrels of years standing made up, village hoodlums turned into humble men of prayer and soul winning. Many, many giving up home and land and going out to the lost around them.

A Recent Letter

Dear Friends:

"We can but speak the things we have seen and heard." Acts 4:2.

For two full years God has been giving us a gracious revival here in Pingtu County. The hearts of the people are full of praise and thanksgiving. One of the biggest features in this revival has been PERSONAL TESTIMONY, the laity going out witnessing to "what great things the Lord has done for them." The Christians have awakened to the fact that their heathen relatives and friends are lost, lost, eternally lost! They are going out seeking them for Christ. Mr. Li, after having been revived and healed, has been a "living epistle." He has been to every home in his big town with the message of salvation in Jesus Christ. There is continual prayer made that whole families be saved; that is, where there is at least one Christian in a family, we claim the others for Christ; we believe that if He was willing to save the Philippian jailer and his household, that he loves us none the less. Many have spread this promise before the Father and claimed it for their loved ones, and praise His Name He has honored this faith and households have been saved.

In many communities where there are a few Christians they meet daily for prayer and Bible study. They pray by name for their unsaved friends, pleading the promise that the Holy Spirit will open hearts and convict of sin,—we believe that people are dead in trespasses and sin. They then divide into companies going into different homes with the message that Jesus came to save sinners. Thus many are brought into the fold.

Karnac says "There is no doubt that the early church won all its victories by informal missionaries." These humble Christians whose 'lips have been touched by a coal from the altar' are going about their every day work as living epistles, seeking to bear the fruit of the Spirit in their every day work, and at the same time taking every opportunity to tell the lost that Jesus saves. Little children, old men and women, people of all ages whose hearts have been stirred are thus witnessing. Is this not Christ's plan? Did He not say "Ye are my witnesses?" Not just the pastor, Sunday School teacher or Christian worker, but all the church, each "Born again" one. Do we find it easier to pay the minister to be our proxy? But is Christ pleased with this? Let us read The Acts of the Apostles, believe the Acts, and act it now. In the last verse in Luke Christ says, "Ye are my witnesses of these things, and behold I send the promise of my Father upon you, but tarry ye in the city of Jerusalem till ye be endued with power from on high."

Beloved friends, are we His daily witnesses? Do

we seek the lost? Have we waited for the 'promise of the Father?" The Bible is full of many precious promises, but this one promise is singled out as "The Promise of the Father." Over and over it is mentioned as "The Promise of the Father." Acts 2:4. He commanded them that they should not depart from Jerusalem, but wait the "The promise of the Father, which He said "Ye have heard of Me. For John truly baptized with water, but ye shall be baptized with the Holy Spirit not many days hence." Have we His children waited to receive "The Promise of the Father"—this power from on high? Have we been baptized with the Holy Spirit?

One writer says: "The Church is not living in Pentecost; the Church stands hesitant between Easter and Pentecost. Hesitant, hence impotent. If the Church would move up from this in-between state to Pentecost, nothing could stop it, nothing. Now it is stopping itself by its own ponderous machinery. Whenever we have been troubled in conscience about our spiritual impotence, we have added another wheel,—a new committee, or commission, a new plan or program. We find we have added more wheels, but little or no more power—hence we worship machinery instead of winning men."

O friends, let us turn back to Pentecost. I have on my desk a book "Back to Pentecost" by Oswald Smith, in which he pleads with Christians for a repetition of Pentecost. If only it could be seen in each church throughout our land. Do we fear this word "Pentecost"! Has it become entangled?

Let us follow the Book, stay close to His Word, and fear nothing.

The Spirit has worked mightily in our midst. Churches have been revived, hundreds saved, the sick healed, demons cast out. Mark 16:20. "And they went forth and preached everywhere, the Lord working with them and confirming the Word with signs following." This has literally been fulfilled before our eyes. Likewise Acts 11:15: "As I began to speak the Holy Spirit fell upon them." We see these and many other Scriptures fulfilled continually. Our hearts are filled with praise and thanksgiving to our Great Redeemer.

Will you bear with me in a bit of personal testimony? The greatest experience that has come to me since I was born into His family was when some months ago I definitely asked for and definitely received the Baptism of the Holy Spirit. O, the peace and joy that filled my soul! My heart was filled with joy and ecstasy for weeks. Not that ecstasy is the thing we plead for; it is the power from on high, the Holy Spirit who is power, even the baptism with the Holy Spirit. But when He comes He anoints with the oil of gladness. Psa. 45:7.

I had been asking Him to help me in my work. Now I stand by and see Him work His mighty works. I let Him pick me up and use me for His work. He uses me for winning others. O, what a difference!!!

"Unless He works, our meetings are bound to be

dry, lifeless and fruitless, but the moment the Holy Spirit is poured out, the usual at once takes place. It is easy then for souls to be saved, backsliders reclaimed and believers edified."

O dear friends have you received this wonderful gift? Acts 2:39: "The Promise is unto you and to your children, and to all that are afar off, even as many as the Lord our God shall call." In all humility, I beg you "Be filled with the Spirit."

Our hearts do rejoice that He has opened our eyes to behold His wondrous works, and yet our hearts are burdened for the multitudes, the teeming millions in this dark land who are still in outer darkness, still bowing down to gods made with their own hands. Will you not pray for us for these lost ones? We know you cannot help us very much financially during this terrible depression, but will you not do the greater thing—will you not daily intercede at the Throne of Grace for the work here? We need prayer help. Pray for us. Praise with us.

Sincerely your representative, waiting for the return of our Lord.

AFTERWORD

What precedes this afterword is a faithful, unedited version of the piece on the Shantung Revival as written by Mary Crawford. The only corrections made were to misspelled words. It is amazing how time sanitizes these past moves of God. What is spoken of with great praise now, was often spoken of in its own time with much criticism. We must keep this in mind as we critique the current move of God; revival always looks clean and tidy years after the fact.

What excited me most about the Shantung Revival was learning that the same phenomena that has occurred during the "Toronto Blessing" was also evident among this great Baptist revival. I have often witnessed people shy away from getting involved with revival in fear that the phenomena will take people's focus away from saving souls. I do believe the salvation of souls is of the utmost importance. Ironically, those who fear that the number of salvations will suffer are usually unaware that the places around the world where the largest number of people are being saved are also where phenomena has been known to occur during meetings. This is true today and it has been true in the history of the church, especially in the last 200 years.

What do I mean by the term "phenomena"? I am referring to such things as: moaning, groaning, crying, falling, shouting, shaking, being prostrated and the inability to get up for periods of time, intense often emotional times of intercession, prophecy, healing, sometimes even raising from the dead, and sometimes tongues and interpretation (limited primarily to the last century). Ralph Martin's book <u>The Catholic Church At The End Of An Age: What is the Spirit Saying?</u>, documents the evangelistic effectiveness of people who have been open to spiritual phenomena. This book, written from and for a Roman Catholic perspective, is just one among many resources, including the Bible, that reveals there is no historical basis to believe that phenomena hinders evangelism. Historical and empirical evidence indicates that just the opposite is true; the fastest growing Christian denominations are those that are very evangelistic and open to spiritual phenomena. These growing denominations do not focus on phenomena, just as the Baptists in China did not focus on phenomena. However, neither do they try to stamp out phenomena or label it as being from the devil. It is true that not all phenomena is of God, some is of the flesh and some can be demonic, but in times of revival the majority of the phenomena is from God.

My intention is not to focus on the phenomena present during revival, however there is a distortion of the history of revival when past revivals are credited for large numbers of salvation and at the same time stripped of the phenomena that did take place. Accepting and documenting only parts of Christian history distorts our understanding of how God works among His people and fosters ignorance as to the natural responses of the human body when God comes close and clothes us in His power. Later generations will then read stories of revivals long dead where there is no mention of phenomena and thus assume that these manifestations are new, when in actuality they have been part of past visitations of God. This historical revisionism is counterproductive to understanding the ways of God and misleads us by presenting an unrealistic and sanitized view of revival. This pattern of historical revisionism, where key aspects of history are removed from teaching, is most prevalent among denominations that are currently strongly biased against most phenomena.

Dr. Jack Deere was a professor at Dallas Theological Seminary and the first to really expose this historical revisionism. In his book Surprised by the Voice of God he documents the rewriting of history that happened among the Reformed Tradition in Scotland. Dr. Deere indicates how later writings stripped all the evidence of numerous prophetic events from earlier Reformed church history. In reality history was rewritten to fit their theological position. Sadly this had been done to the account of the Shantung revival in northern China among the Baptists.

The original account of the Shantung Revival excited me with reports of the power, depth, heart-searching prayer and the challenges to newly converted Christians. I was in awe at the records of people who were already on the mission field but not born-again having a radical born-again experience during this revival. The Shantung Revival records honest spiritual phenomena, like when the Spirit of God would come upon someone to drastically change or heal them and the person would often be physically affected by the power of God; not just their will or emotions were touched. I was surprised to find that all the phenomena that has been spoken about negatively in the "Toronto Blessing" also occurred in the Shantung Revival; except the animal noises.

In regards to the animal noises associated with the "Toronto Blessing" I would like to set the record straight. As of January 2005, I have personally been in over 2000 meetings since Toronto began in 1994. I have heard animal sounds in 5-10 meetings in total, and I think the number would be closer to five than ten. Yet, some people have presented the most bizarre meeting as a typical meeting; creating a false image that this particular phenomena was common, which is not true.

The most roaring I have ever witnessed did not even take place in Toronto, but in Anaheim, California. Let me lay for you the context of the meeting. It was during a conference called Let the Fire Fall. Gideon Cheou is the pastor of a Chinese church in Vancouver, BC, Canada. While he was in prayer one day, the Lord communicated to him that The Dragon had been oppressing the Chinese people and now The Lion of Judah was going to destroy The Dragon.

This prophetic word brought forth a prophetic action of Gideon roaring like a lion. Gideon shared this story while he was in Toronto and many people in the meeting began to roar, especially the Asians and the more prophetic types. John Arnott, the senior pastor of Toronto Airport Christian Fellowship, was not at the meeting.

When this same story was told in Anaheim, California there was also much roaring that occurred. It was very noticeable and interesting to me that the majority of people roaring were of Asian descent; these were the people being freed by the Lion of Judah. Also, I heard more roaring in that meeting than all the other meetings combined.

The sound reminded me of a shout to the Lord, which is an expression that often happens in churches. The shout is believed to be a tool used to gain a spiritual breakthrough and cause the enemy to become confused; similar to Joshua's experience in the book of Judges. The roar, representing The Lion of Judah but sounding in the natural much like a shout, is thought to have a similar effect upon the enemy. I personally have never been led to roar, but I do believe others have felt led to do so as a prophetic act. Enough said regarding the only phenomena not mentioned in the Shantung Revival, that has been only vaguely present during the Toronto Blessing. I would like to briefly refocus on the similarities that did occur in both the Shantung Revival and the Toronto Blessing, and how it did not hinder the number of salvations that occurred..

Now that you have read this book I hope you will reflect upon its truths with an open mind and heart. Note particularly the emphasis on salvation and holiness. I almost didn't reprint this work because when I did a search to see if it was still under copyright I found another book by the same name written in the 1970's. This book however did not include most of the references to the phenomena of the Holy Spirit. It was a politically correct account of the Shantung Revival, without the embarrassing truth that when God moved among the Baptists in their greatest revival He caused people to experience almost everyone of the phenomena occurring at the Toronto Blessing meetings. However, if the phenomena at Toronto indicate it is not of God, but of Satan, then the same reasoning would have to indicate the Shantung Revival was also not of God, but of Satan. I honestly am not willing to say God's greatest revival among Baptists was the work of Satan.

I would like to discuss one other bit of Baptist history. The Baptists of Kentucky had their greatest proportional growth during the four years following the Cane Ridge Revival. The Revival occurred at the beginning of the 19th century and was characterized by almost all of the phenomena, save tongues. This information is in part based upon the notes of Dr. Lewis Drummond, who was the Billy Graham Chair of Evangelism Professor at The Southern Baptist Theological Seminary in Louisville, Kentucky when I was a student there. It is interesting to note that in the four years following the Cane Ridge Revival, the Presbyterians doubled, the Baptists tripled, and the Methodists quadrupled. It is also interesting that the Presbyterians had the least phenomena, the Baptists had more than the Presbyterians, but the Methodists had the most. The Baptists stated that they did not have the holy jerks like the Methodists, but many of them swooned (fell down as a result of the Spirit touching them). Historically, it does not look like phenomena in revival have worked against salvation but rather towards it.

It is hoped that this reprint which I have undertaken, will be an eye opener, and a bridge builder between Evangelicals (Baptist in particular) and Charismatics / Pentecostals. Another great source for information regarding the ways of God in revival among Baptists is the book, The Awakening That Must Come written by Dr. Lewis Drummond, the aforementioned distinguished Southern Baptist scholar.